W9-CBF-509

The World of Stamps
and Stamp Collecting

The World of Stamps
and Stamp Collecting

David Lidman
&
John D. Apfelbaum

Charles Scribner's Sons   **New York**

Copyright © 1981 David Lidman and John D. Apfelbaum

Library of Congress Cataloging in Publication Data

Lidman, David.
  The world of stamps and stamp collecting.

  Bibliography: p.
  Includes index.
  1. Postage-stamps—Collectors and collecting.
2. Postage-stamps. I. Apfelbaum, John D. II. Title.
HE6213.L5   769.56   81-9007
ISBN 0-684-17156-2   AACR2

This book published simultaneously in the
United States of America and in Canada—
Copyright under the Berne Convention.

All rights reserved. No part of this book
may be reproduced in any form without the
permission of Charles Scribner's Sons.

1 3 5 7 9 11 13 15 17 19 V/C 20 18 16 14 12 10 8 6 4 2

Color insert printed in Japan.
Printed in the United States of America.

The Scott Catalogue Numbers are used herein under
license from Scott Publishing Company, the copyright
owner. All rights thereto are reserved under the Pan
American and Universal Copyright Conventions.
Copyright 1981 by Scott Publishing Company.

To Karen
To Lynn

A Word about the American Philatelic Society

The American Philatelic Society, founded in 1886, is the oldest and largest national organization of stamp collectors in the United States. It is not necessary to be an advanced collector or wealthy specialist to join the more than 51,000 active members throughout the country and in more than 100 foreign nations.

The Society publishes *The American Philatelist,* a monthly journal that is the largest of its type in the world, as well as numerous books on many aspects of philately. *The World of Stamps and Stamp Collecting* is the first book offered by a general publisher that has been endorsed by the APS.

The APS offers its members seminars and correspondence courses in philately, a free translation service, the opportunity to buy and sell stamps at special prices, and, for members residing in North America, insurance for stamp collections. The APS Expert Committee renders skilled opinions regarding the genuineness or identity of stamps and covers for a small fee. The services of the Research Library are available to members by mail, and books may be borrowed from its collection.

Information about membership in the American Philatelic Society, or about any of the services noted, may be obtained by writing to:

APS
American Philatelic Building
P.O. Box 800
State College, Pennsylvania 16801

Acknowledgments

In the course of putting together this book, the authors received assistance from a great many people and institutions. We would like especially to thank Fred Barnick, Stan Bazillian, Dr. Felix D. Bertalanffy (for his wonderful photos that illustrate the first chapter, on the history of the post), Fred Boughner, Frank Braceland, George Brett, the late Franklin Bruns, Louis Campanara, Lois Evans, Falk Finkelburg, Richard Gittis, Robert Gittis, Alan Hollins, Austin C. Hood, Louis Hornberger, Myron Kaller, Sol Koved, Robson Lowe, Len Margolis, James Morton, Stephen Pla, Marjory Sente, Robert A. Siegel, Philip Silver, Richard Sine, the Smithsonian Institution, Robert Stets, George Turner, Raymond Weill & Co., Irwin Weinberg, and Svend Yort.

Norman Hubbard's warm support and Calvet Hahn's thoughtful reading of the manuscript were particularly helpful.

For typing and manuscript preparation, thanks to Cathie Ferraro, Cora Jones, Charlene Ways, and Susan Salisbury.

We are also grateful for the contributions made by our editors, Patricia Gallagher and Katherine Heintzelman, and the wonderful staff at Scribners.

Special thanks go to Martin, Diane, Missy, and Kenneth Apfelbaum, who excused an occasional lateness (or two) while the manuscript was in preparation and who offered helpful suggestions along the way.

And finally, both authors wish to thank Karen Lidman and Lynn Greenberg Apfelbaum for their keen interest in the project and all their help and support.

Contents

The World of Stamps and Philately   xi

1. Before Stamps, the Post   1

2. The Stamp Is Invented   13

3. The History of Stamp Collecting   37

4. So You Want to Collect Stamps   47

5. United States Philately   75

6. The Stamps of Great Britain   161

7. The Stamps of Canada   175

8. Rarities   191

9. Stamps—The Investment   207

Philatelic Organizations   227

Annotated Bibliography   229

Index   235

The World
of Stamps and Philately

Serious stamp collectors, or philatelists, derive a world of benefits from their hobby. They are among the world's best educated people, especially in the fields of history and geography. Further, because countries mirror their hopes and dreams in the designs of their stamps, a philatelist can gain an understanding of sociology, politics, and cultural anthropology as well. There is hardly a subject that has not been placed on a stamp.

But real philatelists don't need justification for collecting stamps. They know that stamp collecting can accrue real financial benefits, but it matters little to them, for they have no plans to sell. Even though they may become experts on world history, the historical learning that occurs in the daily process of collecting stamps is not the reason for their philatelamania either.

Philatelists are attracted to their hobby for many different reasons, but almost all of them receive far more than they expected.

For philately portends a kaleidoscopic vision of the world in which pieces are placed together to make a whole. A collection is a gigantic jigsaw puzzle for some, a crossword for others, always missing one last piece, always an obscure clue.

The authors are both lifelong collectors and unabashed lovers of stamps. This book has eschewed the hard sell, though, and has attempted to weave together the historical and the philatelic, showing readers the world of philately. It is a world that most will love, and it is a world from which all can learn.

David Lidman
John D. Apfelbaum

1. *Before Stamps, the Post*

The post was the major medium of communication from the advent of paper until the invention of the telephone. And even today, when there are probably more modes of communication than there is information worth relating, the post still remains our chief method. Billions of letters, packages, and magazines are carried annually. The ease with which the post is used belies the tremendous complexity involved in sending mail: the world's postal service employs hundreds of thousands of people, and it is the result of thousands of years of progress. Indeed, our chagrin over the apparent ineptitude of our postal service is a measure of how much we take mail delivery for granted and how important it is in our daily lives.

There is little record of how information was relayed in ancient days. We do know that Babylonian and Egyptian scribes often personally carried messages for their masters, and the Romans had a highly developed system of message carriers. In the Americas, the Incas, Mayas, and Aztecs employed runners to carry messages. But, in general, before 1550 during the Renaissance in Europe, the transport of messages was an individual, contractual affair. A person desiring to send a letter would ask someone who was traveling that way to take it with him. Payment was by negotiation.

The main reason for the rise of an organized postal service was the emergence of commerce. A banking house with far-flung branches or a merchant with several shops required means of communicating with distant associates. Before the establishment of commerce there had been a need for communication, too, but that need was not great enough to support the extensive bureaucracy of a postal service.

One of the first postal systems that postal historians have sufficient documentation to understand adequately was the system operated by the University of Paris, about the year 1300. The university attracted students from all over the European continent, and the students needed a way of keeping in touch with family and friends back home. Added to this was the need for the academicians at this prestigious university to communicate with their peers at other scholastic centers. A postal system with regular routes was set up, with postal carriage stretching as far away as Sicily, Ireland, Scandinavia, and Hungary. After a time, the University of Paris postal service expanded to include the public at large and was actively used for general communication between Paris and the rest of Europe. The post lasted until nearly 1600, or about 300 years, and in its maturity the University of Paris Post was a business, not a public service. It generated income for the university, and lasted only as long as it could provide competitive service at profitable rates.

Postal service (as in the term "United States Postal Service") was totally alien to the early commercial postal systems. Only in very recent times do we conceive of the post as a state service; previously, especially in the late Middle Ages and early Renaissance, it was a privilege for which, if royalty permitted, the user paid handsomely.

One of the main carriers of mail in this period was the Church. Monks were constantly traveling between their monasteries (the Benedictines alone had 3,600 monasteries), and in addition to bearing their own church-related communications, they also would carry private correspondence. Unfortunately, the Church kept practically no records of its messenger service. Was it organized, with rates for letters in the form of a religious contribution? Were there set schedules that the carriers followed? Or was it more informal, with a letter sender negotiating carriage with the individual monk for a bit of cheese, a warm bed, and a glass of wine? All postal historians can do is speculate. Probably the church carriage of letters was informally done. Otherwise it seems likely that as other carriage services developed in the early Renaissance, the Church would have made a vigorous effort, as it did in other areas, to protect its prerogative.

From about 1350 onward, a relatively sophisticated postal service was developed between the Italian principalities. Italy at this time was made up of a number of tiny city states, dukedoms, and large kingdoms—the country did not achieve unification until the

Duke Francesco Sforza of Milan, who founded one of the world's earliest postal services.

One of the earliest dry embossed stamps of the fifteenth century.

This is a tracing of what the dry stamp looks like.

end of the nineteenth century. In this earlier period, though, Italy was the pride of civilization, leading the world in art, commerce, literature, and learning. Many of the postal letters during this period bear evidence of being carried by an organized postal system. The evidence is a series of what are called *seccos* (or in English, "dry stamps"). These are embossed stampings that show a mail system existed under royal protection. About a dozen Italian city states are known through *secco* marks to have had an organized postal system.

What do these dry stamps prove? If you lived in that time and you wished to send a message, you had two choices: you could ask a friend who was traveling in that direction to deliver the note as a favor, or you could give the letter to someone who, for a fee, carried letters at regular intervals to the place where you had written. This was a postal system. Under the first system—your friend—no form of accounting was needed; the friend would simply carry and deliver the letter. But under the second system, the postal system, some form of official mark on the letter was required so that the different handlers of the letter knew the postage or carriage fee had been paid. Patrons could elect to send letters by foot or by mounted letter carriers—a service that was much faster and probably was offered for a higher fee.

Most Italian states apparently had their own post system, and letters were routinely transferred when jurisdictions changed. Sometimes, however, another state's postal service was allowed limited delivery rights within a postal district. Brilliantly organized, this postal service represents one of the great achievements bequeathed to us from the Renaissance. Postal historians discovered about the Italian Postal Service comparatively recently by searching through old documents. Its existence was surmised, though, as it explains the sudden emergence of the Thurn and Taxis Pan European postal system in about 1550 (which we take up in the following pages).

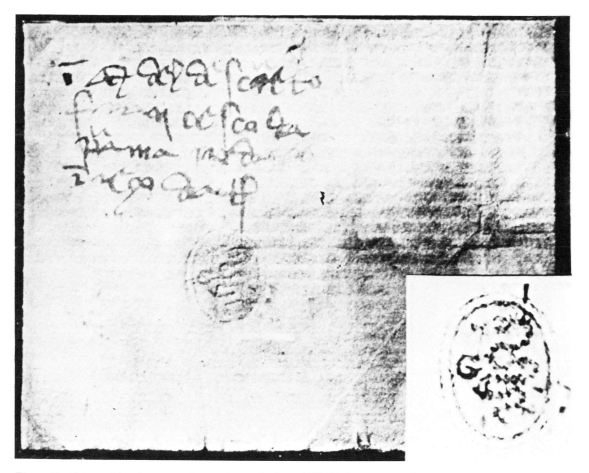

The earliest letter with a dry stamp that we know of—from 1358. Early paper was far better made than paper today, and it often survives in relatively good condition.

A letter from 1406 bearing the dry stamp of two different courier services. It is from evidence such as this that postal historians have pieced together the workings of the early postal systems.

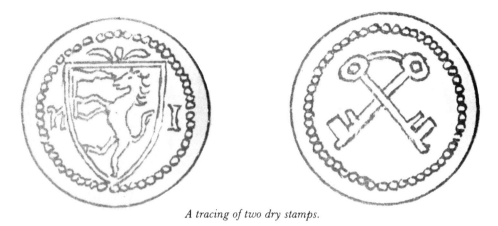

A tracing of two dry stamps.

An early letter dated 1550. The triangles are "stirrup" markings from stirrups on a horse, and are used to indicate the sender's desire that the letter be carried with all dispatch. Apparently, this sender was really in a hurry as he further added "Citto" four times at the right. Citto means "Speed!" The dark stains in the center of the letter are fumigation scars, probably caused by ammonia, as letters were often disinfected to prevent transmittal of disease.

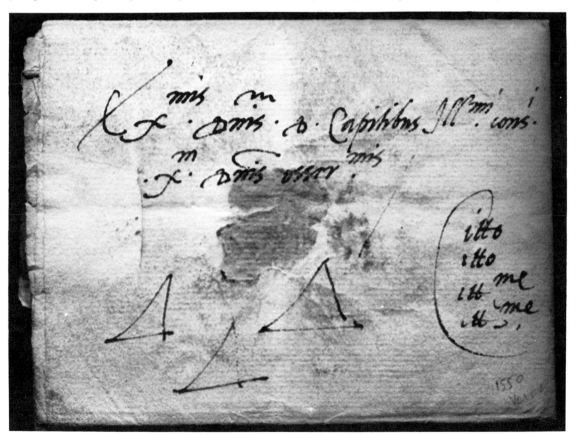

PRE-RENAISSANCE POSTAL HISTORY

Keep in mind that the public posts first developed in the Renaissance were not the first posts in history. Many empires existed before 1300, and whenever an empire arose, the communication system to administer that empire had to be created along with it. The provincial governor of a colony needed to know what taxes were to be collected (as well as having some method of sending them back home), and he had to be informed on new laws and ordinances. In nearly every part of the pre-Renaissance world, empires and governments established similar lines of postal communication. But a walking carrier, running messenger, or even a man on horseback can only cover a small distance before he or his mount tires and must rest. For governmental communication, speed is vital. Hence, a system of relay stations was organized in virtually every empire, so that the message might be carried at top speed all day—and all night, if need be.

So standard was this type of military and governmental communication (the two are usually indistinguishable in pre-modern governments) that Herodotus reports that Persia in the sixth century B.C. had over 1,700 miles of post roads—from one end of the empire to the other—with over 110 relay stations along the way. The Romans, too, had a comparable system throughout their empire, even stretching north into Britain. They called the rest stations for their carriers *mansiones* (from which we get the word "mansion"). The Chinese had a similar system, which began in the second century B.C. and remained fundamentally the same as the one described by Marco Polo about a thousand years later.

But perhaps the most ingenious system of all was devised by the Incas. Their carriers were speedsters, each sprinting along a 1.5-mile route, before their message was passed on to the next runner. In a single day, 250 miles could be covered this way, using over 100 runners. Remember, there were no horses in the New World until the Spanish introduced them; although this communication system was perhaps the world's most labor-intensive, in terms of speed it set a pace that was enviable.

Interaction between the official and private posts is a modern phenomenon. In pre-Renaissance times, carriers for the private sector were not permitted to use the relay stations of the official post, nor were official carriers allowed to carry private letters. The post was designated a royal or state prerogative, and its functioning, apart from the public sector, was considered of prime importance to most governments.

THE THURN AND TAXIS PAN EUROPEAN POSTAL SYSTEM

By the end of the fifteenth and early into the sixteenth century, a courier service that spanned a continent was developing from what had been originally a simple family business. The Taxis family first began their postal routes with a contract to provide service between Crown Prince Philip in France and his father Emperor Maximilian I in Austria. As the years went by, the Taxis family concluded contract after contract with ruler after ruler, linking them with the increasingly large Taxis communication service empire. Before the end of the sixteenth century, the Taxis family was not only providing the courier service between nations but even administering the internal communications

The postal routes in southern Europe c. 1550.

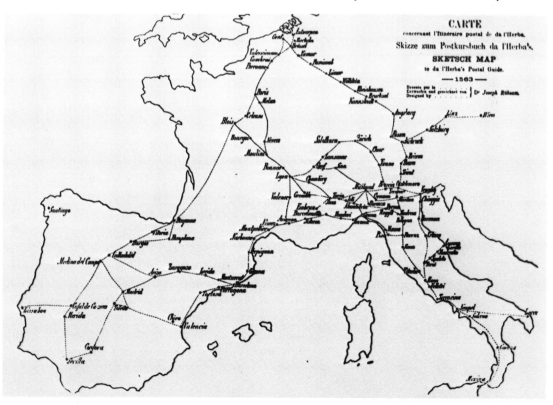

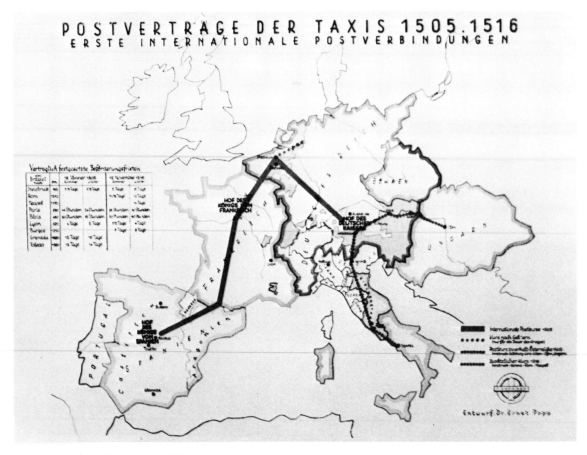

Postal rates of the Taxis Post c. 1500.

within the Holy Roman Empire. By the end of the next century, the Taxis family received the postmaster generalship of the Holy Roman Empire as a hereditary title, and had become knighted Princes of the Empire as the House of Thurn and Taxis.

When first started, the Taxis postal system was for the royal court and government use only. During the early 1500s, in the documents that survive, the members of government are constantly chastised for using the post for private communication and for allowing their friends to use the post for private gain. But by the late 1500s such admonitions do not exist. We do not know when the change occurred, but we can surmise why: the growing business establishments of Europe needed a communications network. By the beginning of the seventeenth century, the post of Thurn and Taxis could be used by anyone who could pay the price.

Today, speed and accessibility of communications are taken for granted. Few people reading these words even know anyone who lives without a telephone and certainly everyone can get mail. In the immediate future, it is expected that most businesses will have a photocopier tied in to telephone lines, so that correspondence placed in one copier can be duplicated instantly halfway around the world. And it is speculated that even private homes will have this tie-in before too many decades have passed, with such conveniences as newspapers being photocopied for subscribers, eliminating all the printing and distribution steps.

But predictions about communications and transportation are

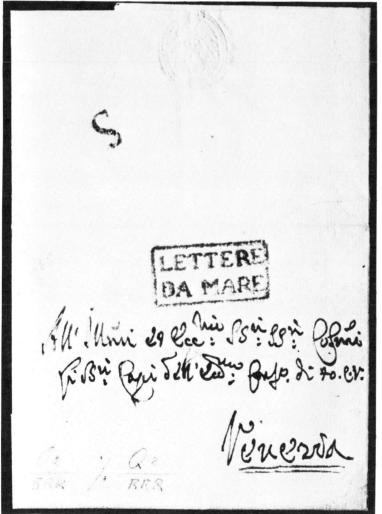

A ship post letter from Dalmatia to Venice in 1765. By this time, the post was extensively used.

difficult. In the 1950s it was believed that the 1980s would see a jet-aged society, shuttling through space for even the shortest journeys. Little did they know that fuel prices and technology would have us bundled in sweaters, paying Cadillac prices for nonpolluting two-seater cars. But while we cannot predict the future of the communication systems of the world, we do know of a long and noble past. The letter that you get today has traveled far, been handled by many, and is part of a network of transportation and communication that is the best humanity could devise these thousands of years.

The first hand-stamped cancellations began to be used in the seventeenth century. This letter was sent from the Ionian islands (now part of Greece, but then part of Venice).

2. *The Stamp Is Invented*

~~~~~~

In 1835, Great Britain was the world leader in commerce. Its empire was truly impressive, with colonies spanning the globe, including Canada, India, and Australia. At its zenith, Great Britain controlled nearly 25 percent of the earth's land surface. Communication by mail was imperative to the administration of its empire.

The British Post Office was run as a government agency, as were the post offices of other nations, with the purpose of producing revenue for the government. At the turn of the nineteenth century, partly because of the high cost of the Napoleonic wars, postage rates were raised rapidly. (A government subsidizing its post office is a distinctly modern phenomenon; any nineteenth-century postmaster general who could not produce a profit for his government soon found himself unemployed.)

A DIFFERENT SYSTEM

Indeed, postage rates were very high in the early nineteenth century. For example, it cost more than a day's pay for an average worker to send a letter from London to Scotland, some 300 miles. Postage on a letter sent from London to America or London to Australia could cost a family a week's wages. Letters from home to travelers or emigrants were rare, and were often written in tiny handwriting, barely legible, so as to cram in as much information as possible for the lowest cost. The cost of postage was determined by various factors, including the distance the letter was to travel, the number of sheets in the letter, and the route by which the letter was being sent. One route was often far cheaper than another, leaving the sender to weigh the benefits of speed versus increased cost. In any case, by modern standards, service was slow, risky, and exorbitant in price.

Letter senders were not required to prepay postage because many letters never reached their destination. Rather, the addressee could decide whether he wished to accept a letter when he received it. If, after examination of the outside, he chose to accept it, he paid the postman. Fraud was common. For example, there was a clever scheme that was used to announce births. The proud parents would address a letter to a relative, using the last name of that relative together with the first name of their newborn. As a result, the relatives would not only know that the child had been born

An 1818 letter from Glasgow to North Queens Ferry, about 35 miles away. Postage 8 pence—a staggering sum in its day—in manuscript plus ½ pence in box, which represents a turnpike toll.

and was healthy (a major concern in the early nineteenth century), but they would also learn the child's name and sex. As the most salient information was already transmitted via the address, the letter could be refused. Address codes of this type were common; although no exact documentation of postal fraud of this type is available, it was well known by and a serious concern to the postal officials of the time.

The practice of defrauding the post office in the pre-stamp period was extensive. To combat this, proposals were made by postal officials to demand prepayment of postage. But because charges were so high and service was so poor, the public felt that the postman would only make an earnest effort to deliver a letter if the post office had not yet been paid for it. Mark Twain reported that stagecoach riders carrying the mail across the American continent had difficulty in adhering to their demanding schedules with stages loaded up with heavy bags of mail. The solution was simple—some of the bags simply "fell out" while traveling across country, resulting not only in lightening the load but also in giving the Indians some reading material.

Abuse of the receiver payment privilege was not the only way the post office was being defrauded. Newspapers were (and still are) permitted to go through the mails at much lower rates than letters. Though tedious, it was profitable work for a person to make a mark with a pin above or below certain words in a newspaper. If the newspaper was a large enough one, a very long message could be communicated by such pinpricks. The receiver of the newspaper only had to read the pricked words to receive the sender's message; then, if he were an inquisitive sort, he could read the newspaper as well.

Another area of postal fraud was unintentionally provided for by parliamentary law. In Great Britain, each member of Parliament was allowed under law to send all his mail free. All the legislator was required to do was to sign the letter, and the post office would carry it. This is what is known as the "Free Frank." In the United States, members of Congress, cabinet officers, and presidents have this right as well—it is a privilege designed to encourage communication between the government and the people. In Great Britain at this time, a position in Parliament apparently did not pay well enough for some of its members. They took additional employment with leading commercial firms and spent much of their nonlegislative time franking letters, which could then go through the mail free of charge. The post office was bilked out of a great deal of money through this loophole in the law and the turpitude of some legislators. Free franked letters of this period are extremely common, attesting to the abuse.

THE EMERGENCE OF ROWLAND HILL

Postal abuses in Great Britain continued to get worse. As might be expected, the post office became an unprofitable and inefficient enterprise. Complaints mounted on all sides—from merchants, clergy, and goverment. Finally, in 1837, a forty-two-year-old ex-schoolteacher and government bureaucrat named Rowland Hill published a pamphlet entitled *Post Office Reform, Its Importance and Practibility.* Hill's pamphlet was scathing in its criticism, but broad in its ideas for change. He pointed out the postal abuses already discussed. He evaluated actual postal costs, and concluded that the real transportation cost for carrying a letter anywhere in the British Isles was less than a farthing (one quarter of 1 penny). Even though the post office at this time was charging over 1 shilling (or 12 pence) for many internal letters, it was losing money. This, Hill said, resulted from the army of postmen employed to administer a system in which each letter needed to be separately rated, carried, and paid for, with a myriad of variables at each of these steps. It took great intelligence and much experience for even the lowest of postal employees to perform their jobs properly, so complicated was the work. Hill had a radical solution: slash post-

Free Frank sent to Edinburgh in 1801; note the "Free" in the crowned circle cancel and the Free Frank signature "W. Boyd" at bottom left.

V R

PENNY POSTAGE JUBILEE

1890

"HE GAVE US PENNY POSTAGE"

A commemorative envelope issued in 1890 for the fiftieth anniversary of the issuance of postage stamps. Rowland Hill is pictured at left.

age rates to 1 penny per half ounce (still four times the actual carrying cost) for any letter posted in the British Isles to another address in the British Isles.

Transportation by this time had become comparatively inexpensive as compared to labor costs. Hill's scheme was to allow the efficiencies of transportation to determine the cost of postage. Everyone, Hill said, must pay in advance for the privilege of using the mail; no more free franking. Hill further advanced the radical thesis that the decline of fees would not mean less revenue for the postal service, because the lower rates would be compensated for by the increased use of the mails. Furthermore, the simplification of the postal service would make fewer postal employees necessary, thereby decreasing costs. Shorn of its gleamy high-speed sorters, zip codes, and registry labels, this was essentially the postal service we have today.

Naturally, this proposal earned Hill the enmity of the members of the House of Commons and the House of Lords. The Duke of Wellington was an outspoken opponent of Hill's scheme, and was supported by most of the members of his various supper clubs. Postmen, as well may be imagined, did not rally behind Hill either. Postmaster General Lord Lichfield stated: "With respect to the plan set forth by Mr. Hill, of all the wild and visionary schemes which I have ever heard or read, it is the most extravagant."* The opinions of the individual postmen, some of whom stood to lose their jobs, are not recorded; no doubt they would have phrased their discontent with Hill's "wild and visionary scheme" somewhat more strongly. However, those individuals who stood to benefit from Hill's proposal (businessmen, lawyers, tradespeople and, in fact, anyone not working for the post office or privileged with the Free Frank) cheered for inexpensive postage. Most newspapers warmly supported it, and after serious discussion the change was enacted and subsequently instituted in 1840.

THE APPROVAL OF A STAMP

"A bit of paper just large enough to bear the stamp and covered at the back with a glutinous wash which the user might, by applying a little moisture, attach to the back of the letter." That was it—the first mention of a postage stamp as it was described in Hill's original proposal. Later he added to this proposal an envelope that would show prepayment, which became known as the Mulready envelope, named after its designer, William Mulready.

Today, stamps are such an everyday experience for us that we do not appreciate the magnitude of the invention. With the advent of the stamp, postal money was created, and because the use of the post office had become so widespread, great care had to be taken to assure that no one could counterfeit stamps (after all, they were

*Robson Lowe, *The British Postage Stamp* (London: The National Postal Museum, 1968), p. 38.

Hill did not work in a vacuum. This is the embossed revenue tax stamp issued by Great Britain for the American Colonies as part of the Stamp Act in the 1760s. It indicated tax paid. Such tax stamps were in common use for years before Hill advanced the idea of postage stamps for letters.

negotiable money). Also, provisions had to be made to alter or cancel the stamp after it had performed its service, so that it could not be reused.

After the passage of the British Postal Reform Act in 1839, a Treasury Competition (so called because it was administered by the Treasury Department) commenced, whereby artists were asked to submit designs for the first stamp. Prizes were offered to the winners, with the best proposal to receive £200—a marvelous sum for an era in which Rowland Hill was offered £500 per annum as Assistant Postmaster of England. Twenty-six hundred

One of the many "essays" submitted in the Treasury Competition.

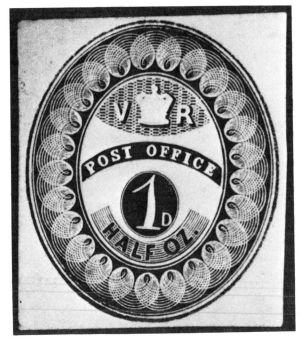

Another very ornate essay. They were expensive to produce, though the first prize of £200 would have made it worthwhile. But even more important, the firm whose design was selected had the inside track for the printing contract!

designs and proposals were submitted, a tribute, as one philatelic writer has said, to the imagination of the Victorians, although one could equally well describe it as a testimony to the creative stimulus of £200. The suggestions ranged from the very crude to the very ornate. Finally, a design using a medal created by William Wyon was chosen. The world's first stamp, produced by Great Britain, first date of valid use May 6, 1840, has been designated the "Penny Black" by collectors all over the world. This is because the face value of the stamp was 1 penny and the color was black. Today, it is the world's most popular stamp.

The Penny Black. This is a die proof of the world's first stamp. When the stamp was produced, check letters were placed in the bottom two corners, with the top left stamp in the sheet being AA. The first row was the A row, the second the B, and so on. Today, the check letters allow collectors to determine which position on the sheet the stamp comes from.

The Wyon City Medal of 1837, designed by William Wyon. It was this medal that served as the design for the first stamp.

A STAMP IN PRODUCTION

Since the Penny Black was first produced, countless technological innovations have come and gone, but the overall process by which a stamp is made has remained constant.

As for the Penny Black, a design for each stamp had to be chosen. Probably the most common design is the "framed head" type, where there is a framed center portrait. The Penny Black set the stage, and it was a number of years before there was a significant deviation from this design by any major stamp-producing nation. When looking at stamps, especially earlier issues, one is struck by how much the stamps appear to be representations of coins placed upon a background. In the pre-1870 period, stamps were not valued as an art form in themselves; rather, they were seen only as

A mint marginal pair of the Penny Black for Official Mail. This stamp was to be used for governmental mail only and was never regularly issued. Note the check letters "V.R." for Victoria Regina at top. The regular Penny Black never has check letters at top and never has "V.R." anywhere on it. The Penny Black for Official Mail is treated by collectors as a separate variety from the ordinary Penny Black.

The early stamps of the island of Mauritius basically copied the style of Great Britain. This is a very rare stamp. Note the error "PENOE" for "PENNY," which contributes to its rarity.

receipts for services due, in effect, money. So why not make them look like money? Furthermore, the early stamp designers were frequently Treasury artists who had worked as designers of coins and bills. They carried their coin-oriented experience with them into stamps.

Early experiments in radical stamp design are prized by collectors. The Cape of Good Hope triangulars, first issued in 1853 by a nation that is now part of the Union of South Africa, are known by collectors everywhere because of their unique design. They were the first nonrectangular stamps issued, and despite some modern deviation into the grotesque, most stamps are still rectangular.

Once a design has been chosen, the postal authorities decide how the stamps are to be printed. The more common methods of printing stamps include lithography and typography. Though neither offers great detail, each offers speed and ease in production at a comparatively low cost. But the most effective, and, many would say, beautiful, method of philatelic printing is line engraving.

Line engraving is also the most expensive general method of printing. This was true in 1840, and it is still true today. Engraving a stamp is a time-consuming process. This factor, together with the cost of engraving, has discouraged counterfeiters from attempting to copy engraved stamps. Line engraving allows stamps to be very detailed, and as the lines are raised, the threat of effective counterfeiting, even using modern photocopy equipment, is negligible.

Take a dollar bill out of your pocket. It is engraved. Every one of the thousands of lines in Washington's head has been individually cut by an engraver working in soft steel. When the engraver has finished cutting the steel, it is hardened (usually by heating) and the result is a finished die. This die must be stamped onto a much larger piece of steel in a process called transferring, which reproduces the die numerous times onto a transfer roll. This roll is then transferred again onto stamp printing plates so the stamp will not be printed in mirror image. Plates can have as few as two stamps on them, or as many as the largest piece of steel the printing machinery will hold. Most United States stamps are printed from plates of 200. After printing, the printed sheets are cut into panes of 100, or 50, depending on the size of the stamp. The Penny Black of Great Britain was printed in sheets of 240. (In

A framed head type, printed by a handstamp, just like the rubber stamps many people have on their desks. This is one of the early Romanian issues and is a rarity, with sixteen unused examples reported in existence. If it were a United States, Canadian, or British stamp, it would sell for over $100,000. As it is, Romania is not a popularly collected country, and the stamp could be bought probably for a modest $10,000 or so.

Cape of Good Hope. These were the world's first triangular stamps. Common varieties begin at about $40 or so. It is well to remember that even the classics in philately can often be purchased quite reasonably. A Penny Black, the world's first stamp, in average condition can be had for under $75.

Sierra Leone. A modern atrocity printed for collectors on self-adhesive paper. Most stamps are rectangular for the simple reason that they separate easiest in that shape.

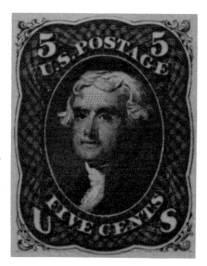

This is what is called a large die proof. On engraved stamps, the die, after it is made, is generally used to make several examples or proofs, often in different colors, so that postal officials can see the stamp and approve its progress.

Progressive die proofs. Here some changes were made between die proof impression #2 and #5: the "PENCE" was changed to "2½d," probably for symmetry, and the lettering at the bottom was made smaller and more legible.

pre-decimal British currency there were 240 pence to the pound, so such an arrangement made accounting easier.)

Plating

The transferring of the die to the plate is accomplished essentially through a process of pounding the design that is on the hard steel transfer roll onto a soft steel plate. In our modern era this is done mechanically, and usually flawlessly. In the classic period of philately (usually defined as lasting from 1840, when the first stamp was printed, until about 1880), transferring was done generally by hand. The extreme pressure that was required to adequately "rock in" the hardened die onto the soft steel produced a

One of the early deviations from the framed head varieties was the early stamps of Japan. There is a frame, but within it are dragons surrounding an inscription. This stamp can be plated by the minute difference in the dragons and the frame.

number of subtle differences between the stamps. This is because no two stamp impressions on the plate were "rocked in" with the same firmness of all minute portions of the design. Thus, each stamp on the plate is subtly different, and because of these minor differences it is usually possible for a stamp specialist to "plate" a particular stamp. "Plating" means identifying the positions of each stamp on the sheet through these minute differences, and the process can be compared to the making of a jigsaw puzzle.

Plating is highly detailed work, and is held in esteem by serious philatelists. One must have a great deal of time and patience (and no children scurrying around the house upsetting things). Two of the most famous American philatelists, Stanley Ashbrook and Carroll Chase, gained a large measure of their philatelic fame through their plating work. Although it is beyond the scope of this book, most competent stamp dealers are willing to show those interested the basics of plating. From a dealer's point of view, a plater needs hundreds of the same stamp, so you can be sure he will help you to learn the skill. (This accounts for the relatively high price of certain stamps, such as the United States one cent 1851 which, though issued in abundant quantities, sells for a significantly higher price than certain other stamps from the same period that have not survived in such large numbers. The one cent 1851 is a relatively easy stamp to plate and, as may be expected, the thousands who plate it require a huge supply.)

PAPER

The most carefully engraved design in the world still needs its canvas, and the canvas of a stamp is paper. There are many types of paper for printing; however, they all have one factor in common—a fibrous weave. Paper takes an ink design in printing (and writing) by allowing a measure of the ink to seep into it. The two major types of paper on which stamps are printed are *wove paper* and *laid paper*. Wove paper is like the paper of this book (technically a chalky wove paper—"chalky" defining how the paper is "sized" or how the spaces of the weave of the paper are filled). Laid paper is made on a mesh of closely parallel lines, so that when it is held up to the light it appears that the paper was put

The difference between a stamp and the old-style hand-stamped cancellation is sometimes slim. A postage stamp is anything that is sold and can be used later to indicate prepayment; in effect, postal money. A cancellation can indicate payment of postage, but it is applied to a letter as it is sold. This stamp, one of the Perot stamps of Bermuda, is named after the postmaster, W. B. Perot, who signed the stamp to indicate its validity. It is worth over $50,000.

This stamp shows a phenomenal double transfer at the top and sides. A double transfer is a doubling of the design that occurs when the plate is made. Usually it is the result of an inadequate entry of the transfer roll onto the plate (a fairly common occurrence) that is improperly erased, leaving some of the old design behind when the new one is entered. Double transfers are an interesting variety of engraved stamps. They are rarely this striking, though.

Dies of the 1852 set of Thurn and Taxis, along with the stamps that were produced from them. These dies were cut by hand.

down in rows, as opposed to wove paper that quite literally looks as if it has been woven. Some form of wove paper is the choice for most stamps because it is cheaper, lasts longer, and usually takes printing ink better. Normally, the printer makes the decision as to what paper should be used. It pays to learn to be able to discern the difference. The three-Kreutzer 1850 Lombardy-Venetia stamp was printed on both wove paper and laid paper. On wove it is worth about $2, while on laid paper it is valued at $10,000. Another stamp printed on both papers, the Canada two-cent green of 1868, is worth $15 on wove paper and $40,000 on laid. Many specimens have never been examined for type of paper so that this is an area where great rarities are yet to be found.

Watermarks

The most philatelically significant aspect of paper is watermarks. Watermarks are the pattern placed on the mat or roll on which the paper is produced. Both laid and wove paper can be watermarked. Watermarks were developed as a form of advertising for the papermaker. When held up to the light, the pattern that was placed on the papermaking mat becomes apparent because the paper is thinner where the pattern is. Stamp producers, in their zeal to foil counterfeiters, placed watermarks on the paper on which stamps were produced in hopes that this additional step would make counterfeiting even more difficult. Great Britain has almost always watermarked its stamps, beginning with a simple crown pattern. The United States did not initially feel the need to order stamps on watermarked paper, and only began watermarking its stamps in 1895 when the Bureau of Engraving and Printing took over from private contractors.

Two United States watermark varieties were used; identical-looking stamps with different watermarks are treated by philatelists, both advanced and novice, as completely different items. The differences can mean thousands of dollars to the discriminating

Although most plates have only one stamp produced on them, there is no reason why this must be so. Here, Brazil has entered two different stamps on the same printing plate. When two different values are found on the same sheet, philatelists call that "se-tenant."

This is an illustration of the second British watermark, the large crown.

collector. An understanding of the techniques of watermarking, which will be thoroughly discussed in the next chapter, can be mastered by anyone with a modicum of patience.

It is doubtful whether watermarking ever acted as an effective anticounterfeiting tool for postage stamps, its original intention. The United States ended watermarking on postage stamps in 1918. Canada never regularly watermarked its postage stamps.

Two interesting types of nonofficial watermarks occur on postage stamps, adding spice to the hobby and value to those particular stamps on which they are found. *Stitch watermarks* look like a series of tightly made stitch marks in the fiber of the paper. They are caused when the fiber mat (on which the wove paper is made) tears and is repaired by stitching with thread. *Papermaker watermarks* are one of a papermaker's ways of advertising. They generally occur on stamps on which the government did not order a specific watermark, or did not use rigid specifications as to what paper it accepted.

Papermaker watermarks are typically broad watermarks extending fully across the sheet, whereby only a fragment of one of the letters of the name shows on any particular stamp. Indeed, because the records of the paper suppliers are often unavailable and because specimens with papermaker watermarks are scarce, students of papermaker watermarks frequently can only assert that a particular stamp is known with a papermaker watermark, but are unable to identify the particular watermark. Unfortunately, the study of these two types of watermarks has fallen out of vogue in recent years. The best collection was sold in London in the 1940s. The major United States stamp catalogue, Scott, dropped many of them from its listing in the 1950s. Still, they do have value, and if you can pick up a stitch or papermaker watermark from your stamp dealer for the same price as a regular stamp, you can consider your purchase profitable.

PERFORATIONS

When Rowland Hill invented the postage stamp, he made no provision for the separation of stamps on sheets. All stamps were issued imperforate, without perforations between stamps, with cutting the only means of separation. Hill did not expect that his stamps would prove all that popular; rather, he believed that his letter sheets and preprinted postage-paid envelopes, the Mulreadys, would be the choice of the postal-using public. He was wrong, probably for two reasons. First, the use of stamps rather than prepaid envelopes—called by philatelists postal stationery—allows the user considerably more freedom in the size and shape of his envelope. Stamps also allow businesses, certainly the largest users of the post in Hill's day as well as in our own, to have return addressed envelopes (called *corner cards* by philatelists). Second and more important, the design of the Mulready stationery was perceived as ludicrous by the English public. Its detractors, led by *Punch*, the English humor magazine, called the allegorized figures ridiculous; even its supporters could only muster faint praise for its busy beauty. Within weeks of its issue on May 6, 1840, parodies or caricatures appeared. These caricatures were sold in stationery shops, primarily as a jest, but some Londoners put stamps on them and mailed them to friends and relatives who might not have seen them. (Today such jests, if postally used, sell for upward of $5,000.)

Within weeks it was clear even to Hill, the Mulready's greatest supporter, that his postage stamp was to prove far more popular than his stationery. But the stamps, because they needed to be cut apart, posed problems for large users. Business firms often would place several sheets on a table and use a razor to cut the sheet into strips, then into singles. This separated the stamps effectively, if slowly. From a stamp collector's point of view, such haphazard cutting of stamps frequently left the stamps with no margins; or, even worse, cut well into the stamp's design.

It was obvious to all but Rowland Hill that a means of separating stamps from their sheets had to be found. One employee of the British Post Office Department said that Hill could not be counted on to support any proposal for postal change unless he had thought of it first. Nonetheless, Hill did come around in 1852, during hearings on the matter, to mildly endorse the convenience of easy separation, saying: "I do not speak strongly upon the matter; my opinion is that it could be useful and acceptable to the public to a certain extent."*

But how should this separation be done? There were basically two possibilities: *perforation,* the technique by which tiny holes are cut out of the paper between the stamps; and *rouletting,* the method by which tiny cuts are made in the paper so that when folded the paper will easily separate. Rouletting is an easier process, and it is found on many of the early stamps. Roulettes can be applied with a homemade device as simple as a modified pizza knife. Many business firms around the world applied simple roulettes to the stamps that they bought, facilitating easy separation. At least one postmaster from the town of Tokay (now in Hungary,

*L. N. and M. Williams, *Fundamentals of Philately* (State College, Pennsylvania: The American Philatelic Society, Inc., 1971), p. 503.

The Mulready envelope. It was very unpopular: its design, which William Mulready wanted to be viewed as an allegory of the benefits of the post, was seen as ludicrous. This example has the added bonus of being used on May 6, 1840, the first day of official postal use of the envelope.

formerly Austria) applied a roulette, on demand, to the imperforate stamps that he sold in the 1850s. This private roulette is highly sought after today and can sell, when cancelled on an envelope, for as much as $20,000.

About the same time, in the late 1840s and early 1850s, several men were experimenting with perforating machines that would cut tiny holes in the paper. The first patent for a perforating machine was filed in England in 1848, and some experimental perforated stamps were issued in 1850 or 1851. The United States began perforating in 1857. The essential problem in developing perforating machines was in perfecting the feed so that the cut holes were made to frame the stamps. Collectors who cherish early stamps know well that though these early machines perforated the stamps, frequently the perforation cut into the design of the stamp severely. Collectors grade a perforated stamp based on its *centering,* with the ideal stamp being perfectly framed within its perforations. Centering is critical to determining quality, a subject we will discuss at length later.

A roulette on Finland's early issue. The little cuts of the roulette knife serrated this stamp. Note the light handstamp cancel and the heavier pen cancel. They did not want this one to be reused.

A STICKY SITUATION

A stamp must be affixed to a letter in order to serve its intended purpose. To accomplish this, the vast majority of stamps are gummed. Some stamps, like the ones the Dutch sent to their Asian and West Indian colonies, were sold and sent without gum. In the nineteenth century, a long boat trip to a hot climate in a humid hull meant that gummed stamps would arrive stuck together and had to be soaked in water to separate them, thereby losing their gum anyway. Sometimes the stamps were gummed upon arrival in the colony; though in India, the first issue was never gummed. The Danish West Indies (the American Virgin Islands after they were sold to the United States) issued the same stamp two ways over the years: either gummed in Denmark or gummed locally.

The gum on most early stamps posed a problem for early stamp producers. In the United States, newspaper editorials routinely complained that the stamps would not stick when moistened and that the taste of the gum was objectionable. The government was in a bind. To make the gum stickier would have meant having to apply it more thickly, which besides raising production costs would have caused the sheets of stamps to curl even more than

The early perforations were usually very small.

they were already prone to do. Gum was applied wet to the printed sheets of stamps and, as it dried, it contracted, forcing the sheets into tight little rolls. Modern gumming avoids this by "breaking" the gum as it is placed on the stamp. Breaking occurs immediately after gumming, with the paper being pulled in the opposite direction from the curl, setting up small ridges or lines that, ideally, keep the stamps from curling. This method dates from early in the twentieth century. The stamps that the newspaper publishers complained about were kept from curling by hanging them to dry in sheets with weights attached at the bottom—a method that prevented curling only as long as the weights were on.

Gum is a major problem for stamp collectors, too. Many old stamps—such as the first issues of Denmark—have gum that just doesn't want to come off. It has cracked and solidified over the years until it has a consistency similar to plaster. Some gums contain sulfur, like the gum used on Germany's 1936 OSTROPA *souvenir sheet* (a specially prepared issue for philatelists that had postal validity as well), which reacts with water vapor in the air to produce minute amounts of sulfuric acid. The acid is too weak to harm a collector's hands, but sheets that have not had the gum removed have now mostly disintegrated. Until about 1890, gum was of such poor quality that collectors routinely washed it off. In the last eighty years, however, collectors have reversed their previous aversion to gum with such vigor that it seems almost as if they are atoning for earlier sins. Pendulums swing; although we will be talking a lot more about gum, it would be wise to remember that gum is just one attribute of a stamp in mint condition.

3. *The History of Stamp Collecting*

~~~~~~

WHAT'S IN A NAME

Stamp collecting began almost coincidentally with the issuance of stamps. An advertisement in *The Times* of London in 1841 spoke of a lady desiring to paper the walls of her dressing room with Penny Blacks. She asked that people send her any stamps they might have received in the mail to enable her to complete the task. It has been suggested by one philatelic wag that she could not have been much of a beauty to want so much black in her dressing room. A second figured she had a morbid disposition. And a third complimented her on her foresight: to paper a 6-foot by 8-foot dressing room would take stamps worth today about $5 million. And she didn't pay a penny!

By 1842, stamp collecting was England's newest fad. But it was a drawing room habit, not a serious hobby. With only a few stamps issued, it could hardly have been otherwise. Women collected in far greater proportion than men (this is still true if we are to believe the United States Postal Service surveys, though until recently men have tended to spend more money on stamps than have women). Alluding to the popularity of women collecting the Penny Black and Penny Red, both with young Queen Victoria's picture on them, *Punch* quipped: "The ladies of England betray more anxiety to treasure up Queen's heads than Henry VIII did to get rid of them." And later, *Punch* again parodied people's desire for "every spit-upon postage stamp."

But these were stamp-savers, not collectors—hoarders to whom each new issue meant as much as the last. The distinction of a "collector" is his or her ability to discriminate and a disposition to search for favorites, preferring one stamp to another for purely personal reasons. We owe the birth of philately to the French who, in the early 1850s in Paris, were the first to really examine their stamps. (France did not issue its first stamp until nearly ten years after Great Britain; accordingly, the supply of stamps in France until 1850 was limited.) These Parisians examined the designs and looked for plate flaws, little cracks, or irregularities that appeared subsequent to the plate's production. Later, they began to search for watermark and perforation varieties.

Stamp collectors were said to be afflicted by "Timbremania," which translates (from the French) roughly as stamp craziness. (A half-hour film on the history and techniques of stamp collecting made under the auspices of the American Philatelic Society bears this name.) But the term "Timbremania" applied to stamp lovers seemed too derogatory to the first French collectors. So, in 1864, in a Paris stamp magazine, George Herpin suggested a new name for the hobby—philately. He wanted a Greek name, he said, so that stamp collecting could be referred to in the same way all over the world. The word "philately" translates as *philos* (love of) and *atelia* (tax-free). Herpin was groping for a way to say "postage stamp" in the Greek language, where it was unknown; he chose *atelia,* meaning "tax-free," because letters forwarded with stamps did not need to be paid for on delivery, so in a sense they were tax-free. Though perhaps Herpin could have chosen a better term, the hobby was ripe for a translingual name.

This is a real gem of a cover. It is a perfect Mulready (scarce enough!) that was used to the United States (very rare), and has an additional bonus of three one-penny black stamps and two two-penny blue stamps used on it. Mixed usages like this are great rarities and very valuable.

THE HOBBY TAKES HOLD

Major car companies in Detroit have long had an adage that their sales are only as good as their dealerships. The theory is that many people choose their car based on the quality of the dealer that they go to—his displays, prices, service, and willingness to accommodate. Philately was well served by its early dealers, especially three: Jean-Baptiste Moens in Belgium; Edward Stanley Gibbons in England, whose firm still operates today as one of the world's largest stamp companies; and J. Walter Scott in the United States, whose firm, after being sold and resold numerous times, still survives and publishes the *Scott Standard Postage Stamp Catalogue.*

Moens began selling stamps actively from his bookshop in Brussels in 1848. At this time and until about 1870, nearly all of the collectors in the world collected used (cancelled) stamps. But Moens had correspondents throughout the world through whom he obtained new stamps as they were issued in mint (uncancelled) condition. Mint stamps were not the fashion in collecting, and Moens in the 1850s and 1860s virtually forced them on his better clients. Those who trusted him did very well, for within thirty years the collecting of mint stamps became popular. Many collectors who had resented Moens's pushiness realized profits 200 to 300 times their original cost. Moens was also a prolific publisher, turning out books, pamphlets, and catalogues with speedy regularity. This interest ranged from Afghanistan to western Australia, and it can truly be said that although he profited from stamps, he loved them equally as much as he did his profits.

Not exactly the same can be said of J. Walter Scott. Though unflagging in his energy, he often thought more of the profit to be made than he did of the means to achieve it. Born in England, by 1865 he was in California during a Gold Rush. Scott's favorite philatelic trick was to buy up the old printing plates of local United States issues. Before 1861, private companies were permitted to compete with the United States Post Office, similar to the way the United Parcel Service competes with it today, except for the fact that the pre-1861 companies were allowed to carry first-class mail as well as packages. The local carrying companies were legislated out of business in 1861, though some lingered on while in litigation. Scott would offer these defunct companies money for their old printing plates, which was certainly found

An early stamp catalogue. Note the date at the bottom. The illustration of the three-cent United States stamp shows a new issue—that stamp came out in 1861. The catalogue shows how popular U.S. revenue stamps were in that early day. Indeed, until the beginning of this century, revenue stamp collecting was often more popular than postage stamp collecting.

money as far as the companies were concerned, since they weren't going to print the stamps anymore. Scott would reprint the stamps and sell them, not offering them as originals, but as often as not, omitting to tell the buyer of their true status. Because they were printed on the same plates, experts rely on color (it was impossible for Scott to match the shade of the ink exactly) and paper to determine the originals.

In Scott's defense, what he was doing was common practice among many early stamp dealers. Ethical standards in philately in general were quite low, so much so that the president of one of the largest collector's societies bragged in a signed article about how he drove around the country buying old letters from unknowing farmers at a fraction of their true value. Most of the stamp forgeries were produced during the period from 1860 to 1910, a time when the ethics of American business in general left much to be desired. Fortunately, for collectors, most forgeries are not at all convincing and can be detected by an expert knowledgeable in the field. But in this early time, fakes were rampant and were often sold as such. Most collectors then did not look at their hobby as an investment and did not hold the pure standard for philately that we do today. A collector was perfectly willing to spend 5 cents to buy a reproduction of an original that would cost $10, a price he was not able to afford. He was not fooled; neither are we. The Scott company began to be managed by an unblemished string of owners about 1900, and that tradition continues today.

In Great Britain, Stanley Gibbons had the good fortune to be born the same year that the first postage stamp was issued. He was not born on the first day, May 6, but that seems to have bothered him only a little. He loved his stamps—and other people's too. He was a collector by fourteen, a dealer by sixteen (so he said), and by 1874 he had moved his shop to London where it still remains today. Legend has it that Gibbons was involved in one of the great stamp "finds" of all time (a "find" being a huge hoard of valuable stamps obtained cheaply). Some sailors wandered into his shop with a large sack. They had been in South Africa near the Cape of Good Hope and had come across, by whatever means the imagination might evoke, a hugh sack of the old triangular issues of Cape of Good Hope proper. There were pounds of them, and with about 1,500 Cape triangulars to the ounce, there was a sufficient quantity for even Gibbons's brisk walk-in trade. No one knows what he paid for them, though many care; some say that the firm today still sells from the famous hoard.

In the 1870s and 1880s, countless magazines appeared for philatelists. Collectors' societies were formed. In Paris, Baron Von Ferrary, a man to whom money was no object, became interested in stamps. Ferrary collected an example of every stamp, and by the time he stopped collecting, there were not many stamps that he did not own. By modern standards, his collection would be worth perhaps $100 million, if so many rarities could be sold at full price at any one time. Ferrary bought *fantasies* or phony made-up stamps that were presented to him as genuine. He was no fool. Though he knew he had been deceived in some of his purchases, his drive for completion was so fierce that he chose to buy the fantasy rather than possibly pass up a variety that might later prove to be genuine.

In England, Mr. T. K. Tapling of the London Philatelic Society (later the Royal Philatelic Society) gave a collection, not much inferior to Baron Von Ferrary's, to the British Museum where it can still be seen. In the United States, John Tiffany and John Luff were examining postal records and creating a reference collection so that collectors could know for sure just how rare an item was and whether or not it was genuine. By 1900, the casual stamp-collecting hobby of boys and girls, and the frivolous affectation of the idle, had changed to philately, the hobby of intellectual pursuit—a hobby that held in its sway alike businessmen, doctors, lawyers, and kings.

PHILATELY TODAY

When most people begin to collect stamps, they are general collectors, that is, they collect the entire world and try to get one of each particular philatelic variety. In the late nineteenth century all collectors were generalists. By the year 1900, there were only a few thousand varieties that could be collected, most of which could be purchased for less than a penny. Beginning about 1893, with the Columbian Exposition stamps issued by the United States, postal authorities discovered that stamp collectors could be a valuable source of revenue.

The stamps issued for the Columbian Exposition came in denominations of 1¢, 2¢, 3¢, 4¢, 5¢, 6¢, 8¢, 10¢, 15¢, 30¢, 50¢,

$1, $2, $3, $4, and $5. The total face value (postage value) of the set is $16.34, a princely sum in 1893 and certainly far more than the average weekly take-home pay of that time. But collectors, though they complained loudly both in the United States and abroad, needed the stamps for their collections. And the post office discovered an increasingly important fact of post office economics—that any stamp purchased by a collector will never be redeemed for postage, representing nearly pure profit for the post office ("nearly" because there are printing and distribution costs included).

This lesson was not lost on other nations' post offices, which, like the American Post Office, have long struggled to balance revenues and outlays. Between 1894 and 1904, North Borneo—a minuscule country on the Malay Archipelago with a literate population estimated at the time to be only several hundred—issued over sixty stamps, far more than were needed for postal purposes. This trend has accelerated worldwide. Today, nations customarily issue many more new stamps than strict postal need would dictate. Some countries' postal past is so replete with schemes to the disadvantage of collectors that even today philatelists refuse to buy their stamps. An American, Nicholas F. Seebeck, in the 1890s, received contracts to produce stamps for Salvador, Nicaragua, and Honduras. He was not paid for producing stamps; rather, he received the stamp plates and unlimited rights to produce as many stamps as he wanted for collectors, and to sell them for any price that he desired. He sold his stamps at different prices at different times, bilking collectors. To this day Salvadoran and Nicaraguan philately lies under the cloud of Seebeck.

In 1900, the *London Philatelist,* a prominent journal, predicted that the number of stamps that would be issued by the year 2000 would exceed 100,000. In fact, philatelic inflation proceeded far faster than that prediction, and 100,000 varieties were known to be in existence by 1930. Today, stamps are printed at a pace that is estimated to exceed 8,000 different stamps per year. Many nations' stamps are never on sale at local post offices; instead, they are brokered to collectors through philatelic agencies in New York, London, and Paris. All of this has changed philately. No one, save Croesus, can afford to even keep up with the flood of worldwide new issues, let alone expand his or her collection backward to include older issues. The situation has produced philatelists who are specialists, which means collectors who restrict themselves to the stamps of one country or one area.

Specialization

Specialization is probably the major trend of modern philately. In 1950, a highly representative collection of United States stamps from 1847 to 1947, the first 100 years, missing only stamps that are known in quantities of less than 1,000, would have cost the collector about $5,000—a decent piece of change, but even in 1950 not beyond the scope of the average serious collector. The same collection in 1980 cost well over $100,000. When a collector can't afford to collect the stamps of an entire nation, the logical alternative is to restrict that subject even more. Today, we see collections of United States commemoratives, which are stamps issued to commemorate events (the first commemorative issue was the 1893 Columbian); or United States Bank Notes, a collection of United States stamps issued from 1870 to 1889, called Bank Notes because they were printed by various private bank note-printing firms; or any number of fine divisions. One of the great pleasures of specialty stamp collecting is the hunt: specialization restricts what you collect so that the hunt remains fun while at the same time proving affordable.

Specialization has become so narrow that collections of various specific interests have been created. One prominent philatelist collects stamped envelopes addressed by famous composers and authors. Another collects only stamps cancelled on his birthday, though wisely he requires only that the cancellation be correct for the month and day, not the year; otherwise, obtaining a new item for his collection would be a major event. Many people collect stamps relating to a favorite vacation spot or to countries of their natural origin. The degree of specialization that one wishes is entirely up to the collector. Philately has no rules and, at least in the Western world, collectors may collect whatever they want.

Covers

Stamp collectors refer to any envelope or folded letter sheet that has seen postal duty as a *cover*. In the pre-stamp period, covers bear postal markings and some form of rate marking to indicate the amount of postage due or paid. In the modern era, collectors have begun an active interest in *first-day covers*. Such covers bear a newly issued stamp and are cancelled on the first day that the stamp was valid for postage. Before 1920, first-day covers were generally not made intentionally and are very rare, commanding huge prices. Today, first-day cover collecting is an active part of philately, and such covers usually have ornately designed *cachets* on them. Cachets are printed designs related to the theme of the stamp.

Thematic Collecting

Over the last twenty-five years, thematic or topical collecting has grown greatly in popularity. A topicalist collects by theme, not by country. Boats, cats, dogs, even infectious diseases (such as stamps commemorating the effort to eradicate malaria), are popular themes. But the list is really as long as the imagination is fertile. Athletes very often collect stamps relating to sports, especially as their days of hustle begin to fade. The demand for equal rights for women has made the worldwide suffrage commemorative stamps issued decades ago very popular. For years, topicals were looked down upon by serious philatelists, yet most now maintain a topical collection of their own. But remember, there are no rules for philately at all. The entire world of collecting is open to you.

4. *So You Want to Collect Stamps*

~~~~~~

For nearly a century now, people have speculated about why anyone should collect stamps. Philosophers used to study the matter; now psychologists do. Surveys show that philatelists tend to be more intelligent than average, but the same can be said for bridge players. Philatelists tend to be curious and inquisitive, but that can be claimed for scuba divers as well. Psychological literature contains references to collecting impulses, but there is little that explains why a person should prefer one collectable to another. Stamp collectors, however, like to describe themselves as orderly, cultured people, who assemble tiny pieces of art for their pleasure and profit. Surely philately is the least imposing hobby in the world. It can be practiced any hour of the day or night, it causes no traffic jams, and it can be as cheap or expensive a hobby as the collector wants.

And Americans love stamps! The United States Postal Service estimates that 11 percent of the people in the United States collect stamps, making it by far the biggest collecting hobby and probably the most popular in the country.

A similar percentage of the British population collects stamps. On the continent, though, especially in Germany and Switzerland, the number of people who collect is much higher, and the Eastern Europeans are known to be particularly avid collectors.

Although no one knows why people catch "infectious philatelis," catch it they do. One hundred years ago, one could easily imagine why the first collectors collected. Those were the days before easily reprinted photographs, before radio and television—stamps were the only window to the world that the nineteenth century had. Printed on those little pieces of paper were thousands of views and scenes of exotic men, women, and places. Just a touch of imagination, and a whole world would open up. Turning the album pages, one could spend the morning in Ceylon, lunch in Brazil, dine in Katmandu, and still be at work the next day. In an era when a 30-mile journey was a major undertaking, stamps were quite an educational tool.

A 1972 United States postage stamp commemorating stamp collecting. The sale of postage stamps to collectors has become a big part of the United States Postal Service's attempt to balance its budget.

But what about today? Despite the social interactions of stamp clubs, which are a great means for collectors to increase their philatelic knowledge, stamp collecting is still a creative way of being alone. A number of husbands and wives collect, but they rarely collect the same types of stamps or use the same album. Often you hear such statements as: "My husband collects United States, I collect Canada." Collecting different areas allows the couple to achieve the individual satisfaction that maintaining a collection gives, while avoiding the competition that might develop if there were resources for but one stamp with two places to put it.

Another reason why stamp collecting has maintained its popularity even today is that it is an orderly hobby. A collection of hundreds of thousands of stamps will fit in albums that can be placed on a modest-sized bookshelf. Virtually all of the million or so stamps and varieties that have been issued have been copiously catalogued. Every stamp has its place. Even collectors who choose to make their own albums usually impose on themselves far more restrictions and orderliness than the album makers ever do. One could postulate that in this uncontrollable world we live in, a desire for order is strong. Stamps go a long way toward satisfying that. Every stamp has its place, and when you are done with your stamps today, you can pack them up and put them away for tomorrow.

Successful collectors, meaning those who enjoy stamps and who create significant collections, usually share two traits. First, they have a deep respect and love of history. It is remarkable today how few people have any knowledge of history at all. Few graduating high-school seniors can name more than ten American presidents, and many know very little about European, Asian, or African history. Stamps are a panorama through which a collector gains knowledge of historical and international affairs. And most collectors have learned well. Second, most collectors have a love of geography. For this reason, they respond to maps and charts. They have a highly developed visual sense, and tend to think more pictorially than do most people.

HOW TO BEGIN STAMP COLLECTING

Believe it or not, no one turns to stamps knowing nothing about them. Nearly everyone who considers forming a collection has had, at one time, a box of stamps that were saved because he or she felt they were interesting. At a certain point, though, the budding collector takes the stamps out of the drawers or boxes they have been kept in and decides that some form of orderly collecting is necessary. When the decision is made to pursue the path of becoming a serious stamp collector or philatelist, the route is well marked. The first step that collectors must take is to become known to the stamp dealers in their area. A long time should be spent window-shopping and talking to the people in the stamp shop. Stamp dealers are afflicted with the same bug as most collectors: they love to talk about what they do. Ask about what to collect, and get a feel for the various dealers' abilities.

The next step is to purchase the basic supplies. You will need a stamp album. Prices for albums range from under $10 to a level that will make you think you are buying the shop, not the album. For a novice collector (though novice is a dangerous word to use as no one likes to think of himself as a novice anything), an inexpensive worldwide album would be the best to start with. Ultimately, most collectors choose not to collect worldwide stamps, as the hundreds of thousands that have been issued form a canvas

that is too broad to have much of a sense of accomplishment. But how will you know what to specialize in if you have never been exposed to the broad scope of worldwide collecting? An inexpensive worldwide album will give you such exposure, and even if you

Nyassa 1898 issue, showing a scene from that colony. Nyassa is a part of Mozambique that was given over in 1898 to a private development company, the Nyassa Company, to exploit the mineral and agricultural wealth. All the company seemed able to exploit was the philatelic wealth, by issuing stamps like the one at the left.

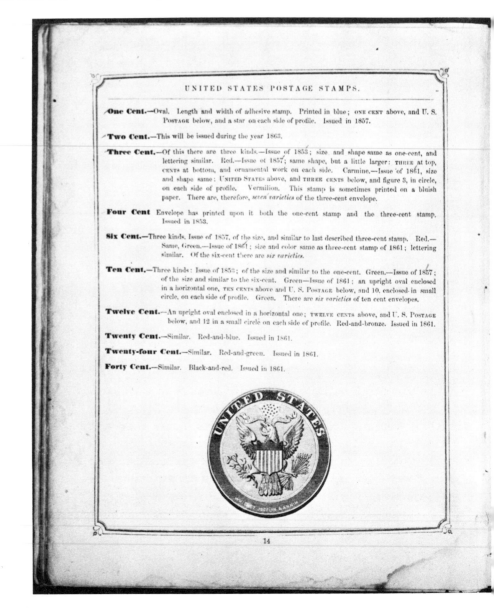

UNITED STATES POSTAGE STAMPS.

One Cent.—Oval. Length and width of adhesive stamp. Printed in blue; ONE CENT above, and U. S. POSTAGE below, and a star on each side of profile. Issued in 1857.

Two Cent.—This will be issued during the year 1863.

Three Cent.—Of this there are three kinds.—Issue of 1853; size and shape same as one-cent, and lettering similar. Red.—Issue of 1857; same shape, but a little larger: THREE at top, CENTS at bottom, and ornamental work on each side. Carmine.—Issue of 1861, size and shape same: UNITED STATES above, and THREE CENTS below, and figure 3, in circle, on each side of profile. Vermilion. This stamp is sometimes printed on a bluish paper. There are, therefore, *seven varieties* of the three-cent envelope.

Four Cent Envelope has printed upon it both the one-cent stamp and the three-cent stamp. Issued in 1853.

Six Cent.—Three kinds. Issue of 1857, of the size, and similar to last described three-cent stamp. Red.—Same, Green.—Issue of 1861; size and color same as three-cent stamp of 1861; lettering similar. Of the six-cent there are *six varieties.*

Ten Cent.—Three kinds: Issue of 1853; of the size and similar to the one-cent. Green.—Issue of 1857; of the size and similar to the six-cent. Green—Issue of 1861; an upright oval enclosed in a horizontal one, TEN CENTS above and U. S. POSTAGE below, and 10, enclosed in small circle, on each side of profile. Green. There are *six varieties* of ten cent envelopes.

Twelve Cent.—An upright oval enclosed in a horizontal one; TWELVE CENTS above, and U. S. POSTAGE below, and 12 in a small circle on each side of profile. Red-and-bronze. Issued in 1861.

Twenty Cent.—Similar. Red-and-blue. Issued in 1861.

Twenty-four Cent.—Similar. Red-and-green. Issued in 1861.

Forty Cent.—Similar. Black-and-red. Issued in 1861.

14

eventually decide to collect only your country of origin, as do so many collectors, the experience will not be a total loss. After all, you will be probably the only one among your friends who knows where Bosnia and Herzegovina is and where Poonch can be found on a map.

Next, buy a packet of stamps. In these days of the newspapers telling us that one stamp sold for $935,000 at public auction, and

Picture of an old American stamp album from the early 1860s.

rumored private sales of individual items for even more, people should realize that most stamps are inexpensive. A packet of several thousand different stamps will cost but a few dollars. They will have no investment potential whatsoever, but that should not concern you. Stamps can be a wonderful investment medium, about which we will talk more later, but the most successful investors learned the hobby from square one. They handled stamps, learned to look at them, measured the perforations, and found the watermarks on them. They even have damaged a few. Veteran philatelists, many of whom have made considerable money as their stamp assets have increased in value, are very concerned over the lack of basic philatelic understanding that is characteristic of some new stamp investors who are entering the stamp world for profit

The Justin Lallier Album. This was the first album produced in the world—it appeared in France in the 1850s. Note that the spaces for the stamps require that they be cut to shape in order to fit into the album. By modern standards, cutting the stamps renders them valueless.

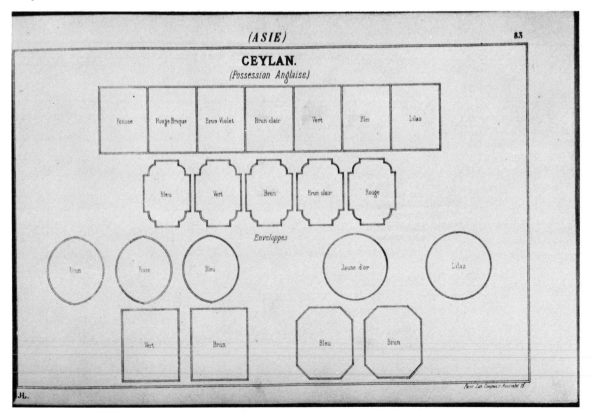

alone. You cannot gain a true feeling and respect for stamps until you have handled and studied thousands of them. Otherwise, you will simply be buying the stamps that other people have told you to and selling those stamps when you are told to. Then, you won't be a collector or investor at all, but merely a follower.

Your packet of stamps will contain several thousand stamps, so you had better buy a stamp identifier. It is hard for Americans to realize that people in the rest of the world do not always write their country names on their stamps in the way we would expect. For example, Hungary writes Magyar, which, not oddly, is what the Hungarians call themselves. Switzerland uses its Latin name, Helvetia, to avoid language conflicts among French, German, and Italian, its three national languages, each of which gives Switzerland a different designation. And Great Britain does not put its name on its stamps at all. Stamp identifiers are available for a few dollars; they contain a list of what the name of a country is on a stamp, with the corresponding English name.

In examining this wide variety of stamps, you will learn to distinguish various printing methods at a glance, and develop a keen eye for color. The human eye can distinguish several hundred thousand shades, though most of us say red when we mean something that is anywhere between purple and brown. Perceiving shades and learning to name them is an exciting experience.

Stamp collectors pick up their stamps with their fingers if they are extremely novice or extremely expert. For nearly all of us in between, stamps are handled with stamp tongs, which are blunt-end tweezers especially designed for stamp collectors. There are two reasons why tongs are used. First, your fingers would tend to bend the corners or blunt the perforations on stamps. It is hard to get under a stamp lying flat on a desk to pick it up, and the slightest damage to a stamp can greatly affect its value. Second, even the cleanest hands have natural oil on them. When such oil gets onto the face of the stamp, it affects its appearance, and fingers can leave fingerprints on the gum—a philatelic sin for which there is no redemption. Tongs should be held in the hand like a pencil, pressure being applied from the thumb to the index finger to squeeze them closed. With experience, once the stamp is held by the tongs, you will learn how to turn the tongs gently between your thumb and forefinger to examine the back of the stamp. Many collectors turn the tongs by turning the wrist, which is nei-

Another stamp album, this one from the 1890s, for wonderful stamps.

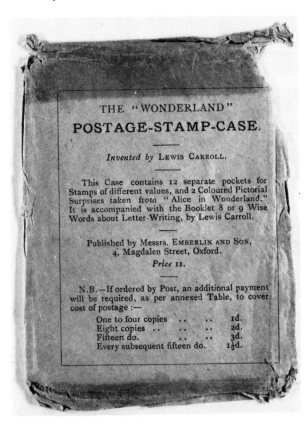

THE "WONDERLAND"
POSTAGE-STAMP-CASE.

Invented by LEWIS CARROLL.

This Case contains 12 separate pockets for
Stamps of different values, and 2 Coloured Pictorial
Surprises taken from "Alice in Wonderland."
It is accompanied with the Booklet 8 or 9 Wise
Words about Letter-Writing, by Lewis Carroll.

Published by Messrs. EMBERLIN AND SON,
4, Magdalen Street, Oxford.

Price 1s.

N.B.—If ordered by Post, an additional payment
will be required, as per annexed Table, to cover
cost of postage :—

One to four copies	1d.
Eight copies	2d.
Fifteen do.	3d.
Every subsequent fifteen do.	1½d.

ther as efficient nor as effective. Some collectors believe it is necessary to squeeze the tongs as hard as they can so that the stamp does not get away. In fact, only a small amount of pressure is required; it is safer for the stamp and will prevent hand cramps. But you will be practicing on cheap stamps until you learn the skill, so don't worry about not doing it perfectly in the beginning.

Stamps are made of paper, and they are subject to all of the advantages and disadvantages of that product. You can drop them. You can bend them, but just so far, and the paper springs back. Most stamps tend to be a little more brittle unused than used because the gum restricts the elasticity of the paper. However, once you have bent a stamp too far, it is creased—forever. As a general rule of thumb, figure that once a stamp has been creased, it is worth only half of what it would be if it were perfect.

MOUNTING STAMPS

The subject of mounting stamps has caused considerable disagreement within philatelic circles during the last decade. In the very early years of collecting, collectors just glued or pasted their stamps into their albums, or if the stamp was mint, they just licked it onto the album sheet as if it were a letter. After all, few early collectors believed their stamps would have any resale value, and accordingly they assumed that they would never need to be taken out of the album. Later, collectors began to use gummed tabs to mount their stamps, which did not come off unless the stamp was soaked. Still, the tab could be cut, and trading a stamp from an album did not mean tearing off part of the page, so this was an improvement of sorts.

Most people would need a stamp identifier for these: the left is Afghanistan, the right, Tibet.

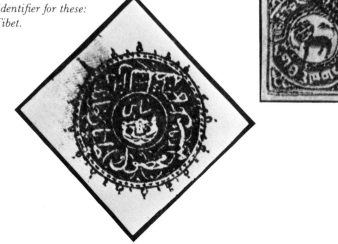

The major invention in stamp collecting was the peelable hinge, which began to be popular just before 1920. The hinge is a small bit of glassine, a nonporous paper, lightly gummed on one side. The hinge is folded, so that part fastens to the stamp and part to the album page. With this invention, stamps for the first time could go in and out of collections easily. Hinges are so lightly gummed that they are quite simple to remove. But never take a hinge off a stamp until the hinge is thoroughly dry. All too often collectors will get a new stamp, hinge it into their album, then decide to remove it and hinge it again. By taking a wet or damp hinge off a stamp, you run a grave risk of thinning the stamp. A good rule is to wait three hours after affixing a hinge before trying to remove it. And do not overmoisten the hinge; a little moisture is all that is required. Your stamps aren't going anywhere.

Another development in stamp mounting that began to be popular in about 1950 was the plastic stamp mount, which offered stamps more protection than conventional hinges. A plastic mount is a very thin polyurethane sheet, closed on one, two, three, or even four sides, in which the stamp is placed and then glued to the page. To retrieve the stamp, the mount is opened. A mount's main advantage is that it allows the stamp to be mounted in an album without disturbing the gum in any way. This is quite the fashion in philately now, so it is recommended that you keep your mint stamps of philatelic value in mounts. However, when beginning a general collection, mounts are *not* recommended. They are expensive (averaging several cents apiece versus less than one-tenth of a cent, for a hinge) and they are time-consuming to use.

The dangers of stamp mounts should be mentioned here. Never use any form of cellophane, masking, or adhesive tape with a mount. All mounts are sold pre-glued, but if this glue should prove insufficient (people for whom this is true are called "heavy-tongued" in philatelic circles), use only glue that is specially prepared for stamp mounts and is sold in stamp stores. The mounts look impenetrable, but they are not. The plastic in the mount is thin, and many petroleum-based adhesives can soak right through it, damaging the stamp beyond recognition. Some mounts are open on two or more sides and may show a tendency for stamps to slip out the sides. If you buy this type of mount, be sure you can live with the problem. Some years ago, numerous collectors taped up the open ends of their mounts with Scotch tape. Their stamps are now worthless as they were stained severely by the tape. The worst you can do with a hinge is to thin a stamp, whereas a mount can ruin one.

Be careful when placing your stamps in the mount. Remember to make sure that all of the corners are in before you close the mount. A small corner bend on an expensive stamp can cost you a lot of money. All in all, though, mounts are generally quite safe, and with a little practice and attention you will learn to use them correctly.

USE OF THE SCOTT CATALOGUE

Once you have decided to collect, and have purchased your album, hinges, and a batch of stamps, you are ready to get down to play. You will need to learn how to use a stamp catalogue. Catalogues number and price stamps, and it is in this way that most philatelists collect and trade them. There are several major stamp catalogues in the world. In England, most collectors use the Stanley Gibbons catalogue; in France, it is Yvert & Tellier; Germans use Michel; and Americans and Canadians by and large use the Scott catalogue.

The Scott catalogue is the major stamp catalogue in the United States, and every collector should learn how to use it. Scott does not illustrate every stamp, but it does illustrate every design type. On many stamps the design remains the same, but the denomination on the stamp changes from stamp to stamp within the set. Every stamp has its own unique catalogue number. The importance of the Scott catalogue primarily is due to its effectiveness as a form of shorthand among collectors. For example, "Trinidad #4" means the same thing to collectors using Scott all over the world, which greatly facilitates philatelic communication.

Stamp catalogues originally grew out of stamp dealers' price lists. They are far more than that now, giving collectors a wealth of information about the stamps they may be collecting. Don't trust the prices in the catalogue, though. They bear only a slight relationship to reality. The prices listed are hypothetical ideas of what a collector should expect to pay for a particular stamp at the particular time the catalogue was issued. In general, stamps sell at a fraction of the catalogue value that usually averages two thirds, but prices can range from 1 percent of catalogue to 1,000

A page from the Scott Standard Postage Stamp Catalogue. *The Scott catalogue number is the number at the left of each column. Next comes the design type number and description, and the Scott catalogue price, mint, then used. The catalogue is a wealth of information; the 1981 edition runs to well over 4,000 pages.*

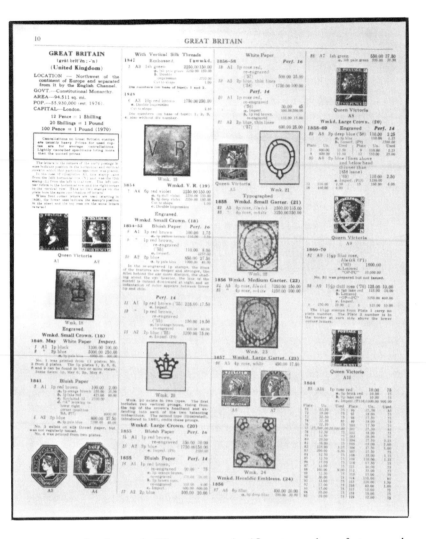

percent (and more). However, a significant number of stamps do adhere to our two-thirds rule.

More realistic in terms of stamp prices are dealers' price lists. Stamp dealers in this country are like dress merchants or green grocers—either they soon learn the prices at which their wares can be sold or they are soon in another business. Be especially careful to ensure that when you compare stamp prices, you are comparing prices for stamps of similar quality. Prices vary more widely for reason of quality than for any other factor, including rarity. A stamp that catalogues for $500 and is in damaged condition might well sell for $100, whereas a $100 catalogue value stamp in excellent condition may sell for $500.

WAYS OF BUYING STAMPS

Approval Sales

Approval sales are popular primarily either for low-priced merchandise or for highly specialized material that is hard to describe in words and must be seen. Approval dealers send stamps out to people who desire them. The customers look over the material, decide what they want, and return the balance along with payment for what they kept. Some approval companies solicit customers in general circulation magazines and even on matchbooks. They usually offer a large number of stamps, sometimes a topical theme, for 10 cents, or 25 cents, or sometimes more. When you sign up for this "loss-leader," you commit yourself to receiving approvals, and you have the moral as well as legal obligation to treat the material as someone else's property (which it is) until it is paid for or returned. The "loss-leader" is of standard common philatelic material (remember, there are trillions of stamps in the world), but would be highly useful to a beginning or moderately advanced collector. So, too, the appeal of shopping at home makes many collectors lifelong approval customers. Be aware, however, that the dealer markup on low-priced approvals (and low-priced stamps in general) is very high, generally ranging from 300 to 400 percent. This is because labor costs, postage cost, and losses are high for the low-cost approval dealer. His average sale is low. A good maxim of philatelic economics is that you pay nearly as much handling and overhead on a stamp worth $2 as you do on a $200 one. So on the $200 stamp you generally pay closer to the wholesale value of the stamp, that is, the price at which the dealer would be willing to buy the stamp back from you.

Stamp Auctions

Stamp auctions are a very popular way of buying stamps. First begun in the 1880s, auctions have become a way of life for many philatelic purchasers. Dozens of sales are held each month, and each major city as well as many minor ones in the United States, Canada, and Great Britain have one or more auctioneers. Stamp auctions nearly always have a printed catalogue in which the stamps are "described." The description gives the catalogue number of the stamp or stamps in the particular lot, an estimated sales value or Scott catalogue value, along with a grading of the stamp. Bids are solicited by mail, and in fact most lots are sold to mail bidders, attesting to the uncommon degree of trust that has developed between collectors and dealers. Of course, any lot may be returned if it is improperly described or misgraded.

Stamp Shops and Mail Order

Most collectors buy their stamps at dealers' shops. There a collector can see hundreds of stamps, all priced, and determine the ones he would most like to own. Furthermore, a good stamp dealer can answer a beginner's questions and help him develop his collection. Mail order, too, is very popular; many dealers issue price lists from which collectors can order stamps. All reputable stamp dealers will accept for full refund any stamp that the collector ordered which does not satisfy him. (A list of the major stamp magazines, with addresses, can be found in the bibliography; they in turn should help to guide you to dealers.)

GRADING

Grading and condition are the most difficult areas of philately for many people since these two factors are so important to stamp values. Every stamp, no matter how cheap or how expensive, can be graded. Grading means assigning the quality of the stamp to a series of words that are part of philatelic jargon. The terms that philatelists use to grade their stamps (in ascending order) are *Poor, Fair, Good, Very Good, Fine, Very Fine, Extremely Fine.* In recent years, some philatelists (primarily sellers), not content with seven gradations and their combinations (i.e., *Fine to Very Fine*), have added another term, *Superb,* naturally at the top of the scale. In grading, as in currencies, there has been inflation. And again as in currencies, the worst inflation has been in the last decade. When another grading rung is added to the top of the ladder, the stamps don't get any better. All that happens is that every stamp goes up a little higher in grade.

Poor refers to only the poorest of stamps, often not even recognizable as a particular variety, due to its faults. Fair is not quite as bad; Good is a bit better. A Good stamp may have tears, will have thins or creases, is generally off center (referring to how the design is placed within the margins of the stamp), and really not of pleasing appearance. This lower triad of stamp grades is not sought out by collectors and would be sold individually only if a great rarity is found in the grade and cannot be afforded in a higher grade. Some collectors on a budget may buy these lower-grade stamps, but stamps from this group are usually sold in large lots—that is, many stamps grouped together at a low and attractive price. In almost no case should a stamp from this triad sell for as much as 10 percent of the catalogue value.

Very Good is generally the minimum grade in which stamps are traded as individual items. A Very Good stamp is usually off center and may contain one or more small faults that do not detract from its appearance. The small fault may be a thin or a crease, but not a large tear or a face scrape (those being major faults). A Fine stamp has no faults, though it may not be perfectly centered. A Very Fine stamp is nearly perfectly centered. An Extremely Fine stamp is perfectly centered and of an appearance that should please the most discriminating of collectors. What the grading term Superb means is not really clear; just suffice it to say that if grade inflation continues, future editions of this book might well include definitions for "Extremely Superb."

Used or cancelled stamps are graded by the same criteria as mint ones, except that the cancellation must not be too heavy for them to be graded highly.

Cross grades are often used to define stamps more accurately. Thus a collector will often see Fine to Very Fine written, which means the stamp straddles the two grades. Such distinctions are valid because it is extremely difficult on many stamps to decide on one category or the other. To call a particular specimen Very Fine

The fourth Airmail stamp of the United States. The left is Very Fine condition; the middle Fine; and the right Very Good. Before you insist on the Very Fine stamp, realize that the difference in price is a factor of four over the Very Good.

might be to overrate it, but to call it Fine might be to underrate it. Thus a compromise is reached by calling it Fine to Very Fine. It would not be too cynical to note that grading depends on who is grading a particular stamp, and that a person's perception of the grade of a stamp is influenced by whether or not he owns it. This is why in baseball the home team doesn't call the balls and strikes. But in philately, the home team does call the pitches in the sense that each collector and dealer retains the right to grade each stamp he sells and to reject a price he does not feel is commensurate with the grade of the stamp involved. So it behooves even a beginning collector to gain knowledge of grading skills.

FAULTS

Stamps are printed on paper, though most collectors wish it were granite. The quality of perfection demanded by collectors far exceeds the bounds of reality. Paper, as it ages, becomes brittle. Any 100-year-old stamp has probably been owned by fifteen people and handled hundreds of times. It may well have faults. Faults refers to flaws in the paper.

There are three main types of faults. *Thins* are areas of the paper that have become scraped away. These usually occur on the back of the stamp, but when they occur on the front they are called "face scrapes." Thins can occur for a variety of reasons, but most predominant is a stamp being stuck down and then torn away, leaving some paper on the surface that the stamp was stuck to. Furthermore, in the old days, collectors would often peel loosely stuck stamps off envelopes, damaging them, but these early collectors cherished the design and cared little about the paper they were printed on. *Creases* are bends in the paper that break the fibers in the paper. Often they are caused by careless handling, such as getting caught in a closing album. But many creases were caused by the original postal users. In the early stamp period, stamp booklets and coils, which make it so easy for postal users to carry their stamps about, did not exist. A woman would simply throw some stamps into her purse, or a man drop a few into his pocket, until such time as they were needed.

Creases also were caused as a result of the postal laws that existed in many countries. In the early period, in some countries letters were rated by the numbers of sheets of paper used, not by weight, so people used folded letter sheets. A folded letter sheet is a large piece of paper which is written on and then folded so that the outside is blank for an address and a stamp. When a business got a letter like this, it was convenient to refold the letter from its side for filing; often the stamp was creased in the process.

A third, most serious, fault is a *tear*. Tears can mean anything from a millimeter or two to an entire portion of the stamp missing. Significant tears, such as an entire corner missing, generally are considered a fault of such magnitude as to make the stamp worthless. As a general rule, small thins, small creases, and tears of 1 millimeter or less decrease the value of an otherwise perfect stamp by about one-half. More significant tears, creases, and thins generally decrease the value of the stamp according to the significance of the fault.

It is one thing to know that stamp values are affected by faults and quite another thing to develop the skills to determine if a stamp does have a fault. Many faults can be spotted by the use of a good strong light. If you hold the stamp up to the light (incandescent, not fluorescent, works best), the thin will show up lighter than the surrounding areas. This is because the paper acts as a medium through which the light must travel. So where the paper

A beautiful block of the ten-cent Pan American. The premium for original gum (og), never hinged (NH), is extreme. This block, never hinged, with original gum, is $2,500; with a hinge mark showing, $1,000; and with no gum or regummed, about $400. Many collectors are questioning whether such extreme quality premiums are realistic when the stamp is mounted face up.

is thinned, there will be more light passing through and the paper will consequently appear lighter. A crease shows up as a light line and a tear shows up as a break in the paper.

To determine faults, most philatelists use a watermark tray. The tray is a small, black plastic or glass dish, into which commercially prepared watermark fluid is poured. It was originally developed for watermarking stamps, and proved so efficient that advanced philatelists then expanded its use to include searching for altered stamps. To watermark a stamp—that is, to determine which watermark the stamp has—the collector places the stamp face down in the tray filled with the watermark fluid. The pattern of the watermark will show up darkly because, where the watermark is, the paper is thinner. Thins, which show up as dark patches not part of the watermark, can also be seen. Creases show up as thin dark lines, and tears as somewhat thicker dark lines. The watermark fluid will not damage the gum of an unused stamp, though collectors should not place photo-engraved stamps or stamps printed on chalky paper into the watermark fluid. Neither type of printing fixes the ink, and there is a danger of the design fading or spreading. A special watermark fluid is made for these stamps.

The use of the tray is what separates philatelic novices from experts. The tray is philately's X-ray machine, and the analogy is precise. It is difficult to use the tray properly, but one who is adept in using it can discern the most subtle characteristics of a stamp. Because stamp values are so utterly dependent on condition, unscrupulous philatelists have for years attempted to alter the quality of their stamps. There is nothing unethical about repairing a stamp if it is to be sold as repaired. However, very often repairs are made to make a stamp appear perfect so that it can be sold for a higher price. Such alteration is exceedingly difficult to tell even under magnification, but it shows up quite readily in the tray.

One of the ways a stamp can be repaired is by what is called "filling" a thin. A thin can be filled by using a form of paper glue or a solution made with egg white. The solution is painted onto the thin, allowed to dry, then lightly sanded so that it fits into the contours of the stamp paper. This repair will make a stamp that is held up to the light appear as if it has not been thinned. But not so in the tray! Though the filled spot is the same thickness as the paper around it, it is not the same consistency. Since it is not the same broad weave as the paper around it but rather a patch, it shows up in the tray as much denser, that is, whiter, against the black background. Filled thins can be as small as a pinpoint or as large as most of the stamp.

It is recommended that collectors who are graduating from novice to more advanced status keep their old collections of cheap stamps, which offer a wealth of perfect and marginally defective stamps on which to learn the skills of the tray. No one would fill the thin of a stamp worth 3 cents, so you can see a good percentage of unrepaired stamps in this group. You can learn what creases and thins look like in the tray, along with how the weave of paper should look on a perfect stamp.

Creases can be repaired, too. This is generally done by ironing them out, using an ordinary iron but first placing the stamp under a cloth so that it doesn't burn. The stamp is usually moistened and the heat spreads the fibers of the paper, causing the crease to become invisible—except in the tray. There it shows as a thick dull line. Tears can be closed using liquid cement; margins can be added; in fact, the amount of repairs and alterations possible to a stamp are myriad. We have just touched on the use of the tray. Most dealers and stamp clubs will give you further instruction. Several universities, including Penn State in State College, Pennsylvania, and Temple University in Philadelphia, gives courses in philately that include sections on the use of the tray. If you assumed that stamps were as they appeared, and never used a tray, you would be correct about 90 percent of the time. But when you are spending your money, it pays to be right 100 percent of the time. Reputable dealers will allow the use of the tray at their office; or if time and space do not permit this (at stamp shows, for example), they will allow the return for full refund of anything that, when trayed at home, does not meet the grade it was sold as having. Be aware, though, that virtually no items costing less than $10 have been repaired, and requesting a tray to view such an item is the surest way of branding yourself a nuisance.

GUM

When Rowland Hill invented the postage stamp, an integral part of his design was a "wash of mucilage applied to the back, which, when moistened would allow the stamp to adhere to paper." In the very early years of philately, hobbyists primarily collected used stamps. After all, the reasoning went, why spend good money when stamps off envelopes were so plentiful. And to spend money on stamps in the late 1860s seemed the height of folly. After all, what could they ever be worth?

Led by the Belgian stamp dealer Jean-Baptiste Moens, collectors began buying unused stamps in the 1870s and 1880s. True, they didn't display the purpose for which stamps were invented (that is, postal use), but the collectors didn't have disfiguring cancellations to worry about. So, they pasted the unused stamps into their albums, or if they received stamps with gum, they just licked them down. This seems shocking to modern-day collectors, but we must all be aware that gum was a meaningless annoyance until the turn of the century. And the hinge, which now seems barbaric to many, wasn't even used by most collectors. Indeed, in stamp papers of the 1890s one can leaf through an entire year's run without encountering any references to gum, except for methods of removing it. Until 1930, controversy raged over whether to collect unused stamps with original gum at all.

"Is it original gum?" may be the most common question in philately today, and it has taken on a much greater significance than ever before. Due to the extreme rise in price of "never hinged" stamps (that is, stamps showing their gum in the quality in which they were issued), great emphasis has been placed on ascertaining the original gum, as this is the only way one can be sure that the stamp was never hinged and that it has not been regummed to resemble a higher-priced commodity.

Determining whether a stamp has original gum is not an easy matter. Many stamps are found regummed nowadays, whereas fifty years ago only comparatively expensive stamps were regummed. Today a regummer, armed with his pail and mucilage, can buy hinged stamps, wash off the gum, and regum them. And many stamps in the $20 to $50 range are now being regummed. So collectors must learn how to distinguish whether the stamp they are buying has its original gum.

Is It Regummed?

In order to determine whether a stamp has been regummed, a knowledge of stamp printing is required. When stamps are printed, they are printed on a sheet of paper that is then gummed and perforated. The order in which this is done is the clue to detecting the type of gum: on genuinely gummed stamps, the perforations are applied after the stamp has been gummed. On regummed stamps, the gum is applied *after* the perforations have been made. If you take an ordinary fifteen-cent commemorative and break it from the sheet, you will notice the way the perforations slightly fray and how the gum does not extend around the perforation tips. On regummed stamps, the gum tends to glob on the perforation tips, extending slightly beyond them and making the perforation tips brittle to the touch.

This is the major test. But now, we are told, regummers are using high-technology sprayers to duplicate closely the applied characteristics of genuine gum. More times than not, they wash the original "hinged" gum off the stamp, and then reapply it, with no "hinged" characteristics. The gum looks original, and is, but it has been tampered with and such a stamp is not as popular with serious philatelists and is sold at a lower price. The best advice is to buy never hinged (NH) stamps that date back to about 1920, which is the period when the gum fad began and when reasonable stacks of philatelic material were available from which true NH material could surface. But, before 1920 (and this is increasingly true for each decade that you go back), a hinge mark is your surest guarantee that you are indeed buying original gum.

But what does "never hinged" really mean, anyway? It doesn't only mean, as some literal graders would define it, "never having had a hinge." An NH stamp must, of course, be never hinged, but it must also be, to use the German term for never hinged, Post Office Fresh. The stamp must never have been touched with a hinge and the gum must be, in all ways, pristine. A technical description such as: "Small gum soak, and large sticky pieces of black gummed paper stuck to back, otherwise NH," means no more than, "Very Fine but for small hole," or "Superb but for large disfiguring tear." A stamp is either NH or it is not NH; there is no "NH but!"

Gum is a vital determinant of stamp value—and probably from today it will always be so. But, consider this, early no gum stamps are beginning to rise in price as fast as the original gum (og) ones are. A perfect original gum set of Columbians would sell for about $20,000; never hinged for about $50,000; and no gum for about

$12,000. It might be going too much out on a limb to predict the renaissance of no gum stamps; but certainly this prediction is no more outrageous than was the prediction twenty-five years ago of the immense rise of "og, NH."

Be cautious in your condemnation of regummed stamps, though. The advent of the modern sealed stamp mounts has put a severe strain on gum. Gum, especially in hot and humid climates, tends to sweat or run slightly, which can make a stamp look like it has been regummed. This is a natural process, but one that is hastened when a stamp is in a mount. The mount acts as a miniature sweat-box, so if you have your stamps in mounts, be sure there is adequate ventilation and that the stamps are kept in a cool place all year round.

PERFORATIONS AND REPERFORATED STAMPS

We have discussed perforations in the printing of stamps. Now we will examine perforations in the collecting of them. Early collectors did not bother much with perforations. They separated the stamps by face difference and placed them in albums. The French set the standard for mastering perforations. When a stamp measures "perf 12," that means that there are twelve perforations for every 2 centimeters. But you do not have to count them. Perforation gauges can be purchased: these are made with lines and holes that show, when a stamp is placed on them, the precise gauge of the perforations.

Modern collectors pay a great deal of attention to perforations and they are a major determinant of quality. All of the perforation teeth are expected to be intact. Should any perforation tip fall below half of its expected length, as judged by the perforations around it, the stamp is referred to as having "nibbed perfs." Should the perforation tooth be missing entirely, the stamp is said to have a "short" or "pulled perf." Nibbed perfs generally

A reperforated two-cent Transmississippi of the United States. Note how the right row does not line up with its opposite and how flat the edges of the perf tips are. Once straight edges were quite common. Now, because collectors do not like them, most have been reperfed and straight edges have become quite scarce.

decrease the value of an otherwise perfect stamp by about 25 percent, while short perfs can decrease the value by up to 50 percent.

United States stamps up through the 1930s were produced on a press that has been termed a *flat press*. A large sheet of paper is placed on the press, and the plate comes down to print the stamps. While this is an effective method of printing, it is not very speedy, as each sheet of paper has to be placed on the press individually and then taken off again. In an era when stamp needs were small, this did not matter, and a good press manned by experienced printers produced enough stamps. In the late 1920s, the United States began to use a much speedier press, the *rotary press,* which prints using a curved plate on a continously fed sheet of paper. Rotary printing eliminates the need for each piece of paper to be placed on the press individually. The long roll of printed stamps is then gummed, perforated, and cut into sheets.

All of this is germane to perforations because when a single sheet of paper is used to print a stamp, it is not necessary to perforate the edges of that sheet when the perforating step of the stamp production process comes along. The flat press–printed sheet is placed in the perforator, and generally the outside edges are left imperforate. These stamps with imperforate sides are called "straight edges." Due to highly technical variances in printing on a flat press, straight edges can exist on one, two, or no sides, though data exists to tell us which is the case for each stamp issue. United States stamps were printed on a flat press until the late 1920s (and occasionally after that) and so exist with straight edges.

Straight edge stamps are not desired by collectors, for the reason that only the Great Collector knows, even though they are far scarcer than the fully perforated stamps. Accordingly, the morally feeble have discovered another way to line their pockets: buy a perforating machine, buy straight edge stamps, and perforate the side or sides that are straight edged.

Fortunately, reperforated stamps (as they are called by collectors) are generally not too difficult to tell. The first clue comes from examining the stamp carefully. Do all the rows of perforations seem to be even or does one of the rows cut at an angle? Government-applied rows are always parallel to each other, and it is surprising how few reperfers obey even this simple rule. Second, look at the perforation teeth themselves. When a normally printed stamp is torn apart along the perforations, it is never done completely cleanly. Most perforation teeth fray slightly, and there is a tendency for one or more teeth to be slightly longer or shorter than the others. Avoid stamps where the perforations on the side look flat, that is, where the perf tips all end at one place. Reperfers do their work against the flat, straight-edged side, so reperfed copies usually look this way.

GETTING WHAT YOU PAY FOR

There should be some anxiety on the part of a new collector that he or she is getting stamps of sufficient quality for the price that is paid. This is not to say that collectors should buy only stamps in exceptional quality; rather, a stamp in nearly any quality is desirable, providing it is accurately graded and priced at what it is really worth. Quality is the single determinant in stamp prices, and you must be sure that you are getting what you pay for.

This sounds nice, but how can it be done? First of all, anyone seriously considering committing a portion of his resources to philatelic items should critically examine the dealers he is planning to do business with. A collector should only do business with one firm if, after trying several, he concludes that this one firm is reliable and has competitive prices. Few people would send their children to a private school because it is convenient, and few choose a doctor based on price.

Most communities in the United States have stamp clubs. Their meeting times and places can be found in the Sunday philatelic columns of the general circulation newspapers of your town. And you should go! You should also join a national philatelic society or subscribe to a national philatelic magazine (lists of these are given starting on page 227).

Once you go to a club meeting, don't be passive. Ask questions. "Dealer X—is he reliable?" "How about Dealer Y?" While keeping in mind that probably no dealer in the world has pleased all of his customers (and indeed, some people are virtually unpleasable), one can gain a sense of the prevailing informed philatelic sentiment toward the local stamp shops.

Next, shop the shops. Prices can vary a great deal in stamps. Sometimes in a town with quite a few dealers, pricing an item around can save you as much as 20 percent for identical quality.

This is because most dealers find themselves a niche for which they are known—be it United States mint singles, British Commonwealth, Canada, or any of a host of other specialties and sub-specialties. If the dealer buys a collection that is not in his niche, chances are his prices will be somewhat lower for this material as his call for it is not as great as for his specialty.

When you shop stamp dealers, make sure you shop quality. Look at how the dealer grades his stamps. Some dealers call Very Fine what another dealer calls Fine. Unfortunately, there is no standardized grading system in philately, so each dealer is free to grade his stamps as he wishes. Some are conservative graders and some are liberal graders. Ultimately, however, the final grader of each philatelic item is the prospective purchaser. It doesn't matter what the merchant calls it, it has to meet the standards of the buyer. This is why some dealers' Fine grades sell for more than other dealers' Very Fine grades. But you should try to deal with conservative graders, for it is with them that most serious and knowledgeable collectors do their business.

Check the prices you pay, too. There are hundreds of stamp dealers in this country who publish price lists and auction catalogues (with prices realized). A wise collector will see to it that he gets some of these publications so that he knows what a given item is selling for in other areas. Remember, too, that most philatelic business is done by mail, so don't be adverse to considering this method of purchasing. Reputable mail dealers guarantee everything they sell.

Does your dealer belong to the American Stamp Dealers Association? The ASDA is a group of well over 1,000 stamp dealers, who have banded together in an effort to promote high standards of stamp dealing. This is a high-minded and noble effort, but it was done mostly for reasons of self-interest. Collectors who are bilked by stamp dealers (and this happens in stamps as it does in all businesses) are less likely to continue in the hobby than collectors who have satisfactory relations with their philatelic suppliers. The ASDA promotes stamp collecting and polices the ethical conduct of its members. It is difficult to gain admission to the ASDA, and any member can be dropped as the result of a reasonable complaint from a collector. Any collector may make a complaint against a dealer, and the dealer is required to respond to the ASDA in writing. If the case has a valid basis, it is remanded to the ASDA counsel or to the Ethics Committee. The dealer can be required to make restitution, and he may be suspended or expelled. This is a remedy that collectors can resort to without the burden of legal aid. You should also be advised, however, that there are a small number of impeccably reputable dealers who do not hold ASDA membership, so lack of ASDA membership should not in itself disqualify a dealer from your consideration. A list of ASDA members can be obtained from the ASDA general office (the address is given in the list of philatelic organizations at the end of this book).

The American Philatelic Society (APS) is an organization with nearly 100 years of history. It has over 50,000 members, is devoted to the promotion of philately, and besides printing an excellent monthly magazine, one of its many services revolves around protecting collectors. Membership in the APS is highly recommended. Many stamp dealers in this country grant immediate credit to a limited amount to APS members. This is quite useful when ordering stamps by mail. The Society of Philatelic Americans (SPA), though smaller than the APS, provides many of the same services.

The smallest crease, the tiniest thin, a minute repair, or a regumming job, however expert, all greatly affect the value of a stamp. And unfortunately, even knowledgeable philatelists sometimes miss problems like these. In the United States there are three major certifying boards: the Philatelic Foundation (PFC), the American Philatelic Expertization Service (APES), and the Society of Philatelic Americans Expert Service (SPA). Stamps can be sent to these groups, and for a usually modest fee, they will examine them and return them with a certificate. The certificate lists whether or not the stamp is genuine, and if it is, whether it has any faults.

Most stamps are not sold with certificates, but this in no way impugns the stamp's genuineness. Rather, the certification process is a time-consuming one, often taking three months or more, and most dealers cannot afford to tie up inventory for that long. However, no reputable dealer will refuse to allow you the right to send off for a certificate on any stamp bought from him, with the right to return the stamp if it does not meet the level at which it was sold. The generally accepted rule is that certification costs are paid by the purchaser if the stamp is certified as the quality in which it was sold, and by the seller if the stamp is certified not as

No. 90 066   August 15, 1980   *A Philatelic Foundation Certificate.*

THE PHILATELIC FOUNDATION

270 MADISON AVENUE
NEW YORK, N.Y. 10016

EXPERT COMMITTEE

We have examined the enclosed item submitted by the applicant described as follows:

Country __USA__ Issue __1867__ Denomination __2¢__

Color __black__ Cat. No. __84__

<small>Brief description or additional information   All Catalogue numbers are Scott's unless otherwise specified.</small>

On cover with New York City, Mar. 31 cds.

of which a photograph is attached and are of the opinion

that the stamp, Scott 87, E grill, is gen-

uinely used on this cover with a blue town

cancellation.-------------------------------

For The Expert Committee
Chairman

submitted by _____

described and must be returned. Be advised that the certificate does not grade the stamp (e.g., Very Fine, Fine, etc.); rather, it will ascertain genuineness, enumerate faults, and, for a mint stamp, tell whether or not it has original gum, but not whether it has ever been hinged.

A short plea for the stamp dealer is in order here. The minutiae involved in grading and describing philatelic material is so complex that, on occasion, even the most reputable philatelic houses make mistakes. Should this happen to you and should you order or bid on and receive a misdescribed stamp, approach the dealer unantagonistically so that he can void the sale. There is nothing more tragic than a collector who views every misdescribed stamp as a personal affront, and who sees himself as the last bastion of philatelic ethics and moral righteousness in an otherwise sordid world.

5. *United States Philately*

The lessons learned by Great Britain were not lost on America. This was a huge country, sprawling out by 1847 as far as California. The population density in the West was exceedingly low, although because of rich natural resources there were a good number of small and medium-sized urban centers. The post office was required to serve all these small and medium towns, and, to complicate matters, the western states lobbied actively for cheap postage. In 1847, the United States government issued its first postage stamp, and at the same time reduced postage rates substantially.

THE FIRST UNITED STATES STAMPS

Collectors of United States stamps usually collect according to the numbering system of the Scott catalogue. The Scott catalogue numbers each stamp chronologically, beginning with the 1847

The autograph of Benjamin Franklin. Franklin was the first American Postmaster General and had the Free Frank. When he franked letters, he used "B Free Franklin." Here his signature is just on a letter (if you can say "just" when the price tag is over $2,500). Stamp collectors collect autographs of famous postal people.

five-cent Franklin as number 1. Each stamp that is considered a major collecting type is given a number, or a number and a capital letter. Subtypes of each stamp are given a small alphabetical letter after the major number. Thus the brown shade of America's first stamp is #1; the shade varieties that are variations of brown are called #1a, #1b, and #1c.

The first United States stamps were issued imperforate and were printed by Rawdon, Wright, Hatch & Edson, from stock dies held by the firm. The cost of line-engraving individual dies was great, and it was only natural that such double duty by the dies was used. The five-cent and ten-cent 1847 stamps were valid for postage on July 1, 1847, and were supposed to be in post offices that day. No first-day covers are known, and any covers cancelled during the entire month of July are very rare.

The five-cent 1847 stamp bears the portrait of Benjamin Franklin, the first Postmaster General of the United States. In terms of the quality of printing, though certainly not of design, this is probably the worst American stamp. The design was well chosen and properly engraved, but the impressing of the stamp onto the paper was usually poorly done. The high quality of the printing of the ten-cent 1847 attests to the expertise of the printers, so there must be other causes for the poor quality of the five cent. It has been theorized that the ink from which the five cent was printed severely corroded the plate. This theory would explain the general mottled impression that this stamp has. Strong, clear impressions command a substantial premium.

Five cent 1847, Scott #1. This first United States postage stamp is very rare with all four margins. When it has four margins, it is rated Very Fine and commands a substantial premium.

The five-cent stamp paid the regular first-class postage rate under 300 miles and the ten cent paid the postage rate over 300 miles. Covers are known with both five-cent and ten-cent stamps on them, generally paying for an overweight letter, but these are great rarities. Furthermore, five-cent and ten-cent 1847 stamps could be placed on letters posted from Canada. In this early period, senders could not mail prepaid letters across national boundaries, as each country wanted to collect the postage that was due for its part of the journey. However, some business firms in Canada with important American customers would pay the Canadian postage and put an American stamp on the letter to prevent the letter from going postage due. Such items are rare.

Photograph of a Rawdon Wright, Hatch & Edson printed bank note showing the stock dies used for the ten cent 1847. Note that Washington's picture on the note is the same cut as used on the first stamps. Engraving these tiny portraits took weeks, sometimes months. Often an engraving firm could not show a profit until it had a stock of these dies to use, as the cost of engraving each job completely was prohibitive.

A stampless cover from California during the Gold Rush days, showing a happy prospector panning for gold.

A cover bearing the five cent 1847, cancelled by pen.

The ten cent 1847, a used pair.

One area of concern for collectors who seek to acquire America's first two stamps in mint, that is uncancelled, condition lies in the danger of "cleaned" stamps. In this early period, most large post offices had cancelling devices, but it was unclear to their postmasters whether they were to use the canceller to cancel the stamp or to use the machine to mark the date on the letter and then cancel the stamp by pen strokes. Small towns often had no cancelling devices at all and pen and ink was readily used. A large percentage of the #1s and the #2s were cancelled by pen, and over the years some collectors, dealers, and just plain hucksters have "cleaned" the cancellation off the stamp. The details of cleaning are complex, involving the use of both heat and acids. The stamp appears to be unused, though of course it is not. And with unused five-cent and ten-cent 1847 stamps selling at fifteen times the used price, a buyer must exercise care. Most serious collectors and all competent professionals can tell a cleaned stamp from an original, unused one. Under high magnification the pen mark can never be completely eradicated. Still, it would be wise to insist on a certificate of authenticity (see page 73) before buying an unused 1847 stamp.

But this is largely academic because most collectors collect these first two stamps used. The deep rich color of the stamps lends itself well to cancelling, red cancellations being the most common. Most collectors of United States stamps collect used stamps to 1890 and unused after that, though this is often an economic imperative rather than an aesthetic choice. Unused stamps before 1890 are prohibitively expensive.

Prices of the United States' first two stamps have been rising steeply, quadrupling in the decade of the 1970s.

THE 1851s

In 1851, another general postage rate reduction was deemed in order. The price of sending a drop letter (a letter dropped off at a post office for someone else to pick up) was reduced from 2 cents to 1 cent. Furthermore, the first-class rate was lowered from 5 cents to 3 cents, and a five-cent stamp was issued for use on letters that traveled by ship. A ten-cent stamp was issued for mail sent from the East to the West coast. A twelve-cent stamp for foreign letters rounded out the set. All values are imperforate.

A ten-cent 1847 cover called "Pensacola, F.T.," standing for Florida Territory. Florida became a state in 1845; they just didn't change the cancellation.

The One Cent 1851 (#5, 6, 7, 8, 8A, 9)

This is one of American philately's most difficult and most interesting stamps. All of the one-cent 1851 stamps look alike to the casual collector. However, there are several types that philatelists recognize as different stamps. The differences were caused when the stamp die was transferred to the transfer roll. Individual cuttings by the engraver of each position on the plate would be an endless task. And a die cannot be directly transferred to the plate because both the die and the plate need to be in reverse. A transfer roll is the intermediate step. So this form of exact reproduction was developed, and it has remained the most effective security printing method to this day. On the one cent 1851, the types of the stamp are due to varieties caused during the transfer of the die to the plate, and by plate wear.

Not all collectors care to differentiate among the various types, as these minutely different stamps are called. Still with the rarest type, Type I, selling at about $10,000, and the most common type selling at $40, it makes sense to learn. The types of the one cent 1851 are the hardest part of United States philately; once you master them, everything else is relatively easy. Remember, of course, that most of philately deals with minutiae, and each collector can decide for himself how specialized he wants to become. This degree of specialization is one of the watersheds that separates advanced from casual collectors.

A proof of the rare Type I (above) and the original die for the frame (below). Both show the complete frame design.

The Types of the One Cent 1851

• Type I (#5) The *complete design* as it was engraved on the die. This is found in only one position on the plate. The ornaments are complete at the bottom, top, and sides. Though 30,000 were estimated printed, only a tiny fraction are known to philatelists—there are probably quite a few left to be discovered. This stamp is worth anywhere from $1,000 to $10,000, depending on condition.

• Type Ia (#6) Similar to Type I except that the top frameline is partially cut away.

• Type II (# 7) This is one of the more common types. It has parts of the design missing at its top and bottom, but the lines below "ONE CENT" and above "U.S. POSTAGE" are always intact.

• Type III (#8) There are major parts of the design missing at the top and bottom, always including the lines below "ONE CENT" and above "U.S. POSTAGE."

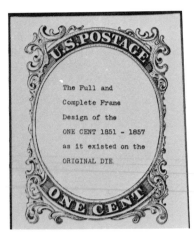

The Full and
Complete Frame
Design of the
ONE CENT 1851 - 1857
as it existed on the
ORIGINAL DIE.

- Type IIIa (#8A) The line below "ONE CENT" *or* the line above "U.S. POSTAGE" is broken, but not both.
- Type IV (#9) As plate one started to wear, the lines at the top and bottom began to disappear, so they were recut: this means that an engraver went to the plate and individually strengthened the lines. The effect shows up as dark lines above "U.S. POSTAGE" and/or below "ONE CENT" on the Type IV.

A Type Ia #6; note the way the top part of the design is partially cut away. The bottom part of the stamp is missing, but philatelists can tell it is the proper type by plating.

A Type II #7; note that parts of the ornaments are missing at top and at bottom.

A beautiful strip of three paying the three-cent first-class postage rate. This cover is called an advertising cover because of the company advertising return address at the left. Such advertising covers are quite popular among collectors and can sometimes be incredibly ornate.

A Type IV #9; note the recut darker lines above "U.S. POSTAGE" and below "ONE CENT."

A proof example of the three cent 1851.

The one-cent 1851 stamp is one of America's most popular specialty stamps. There are many different types, a fascinating array of cancels, and this stamp is easier to plate (see page 27) than any other American stamp. It is difficult to find good four-margin examples of this stamp and they command premiums.

The Three Cent 1851 (#10 and #11)

This stamp paid the common letter rate that was reduced from 5 cents to 3 cents on July 1, 1851. There are two main varieties of this stamp. The #10, known from 1851 printings of the stamp, is a shade variety. The color is described in the Scott catalogue as copper brown or orange brown (and here Scott does a far better job of color description than is often the case). The #10 has the color of a well-worn penny and came from early printings of the stamp. The #11, which comes in numerous shades itself, is every other red brown shade except copper or orange brown. This is another popular specialist stamp. Good copies of the #11 still sell for under $10, and even when unused with original gum, they don't often top $100. So a collector could specialize in just this stamp and still send his children to college. Millions of these stamps were issued, though considerably less than that survive. The number of stamps issued of any particular design is generally known by philatelists, as over the years philatelic students have dug out the information by scanning postal records. But predicting a survival rate is considerably more difficult. In this early period, reliable estimates indicate that only a small fraction of the issued number of common rate stamps have survived and now exist in collectors' hands. Of higher rate stamps, more were usually saved, probably because the receivers kept them as novelties.

The Five Cent 1851 (#12)

Many collectors believe this is the most beautifully engraved United States stamp. It was issued to pay the internal United States postage rate on letters destined for overseas. The rate included the 3 cents internal rate and a 2-cent ship letter fee. With a few exceptions, letters of this period required that postage be paid to all nations involved in its carriage, not just the originating nation, as is the case today. Accordingly, most people paid the postage to the port, and let the addressee pick up the balance. The stamps were printed closely together—so close that copies showing all four margins are very rare. The number printed has been estimated at 150,000, so that probably fewer than 10,000 exist today in philatelists' hands. Mint examples are rarities.

A stamp of the five cent 1851 #12.

A very rare block of four of the five cent 1851, with a manuscript, or pen, cancel.

The Ten Cent 1851

This stamp, picturing George Washington, was issued to pay the first-class postage rate between the East and West coasts. The ten cent is a stamp much like the one cent; it has four types in its imperforate printing.

• Type I (#13) has a full plume at right and bottom, and a partial plume at left. The line below "TEN CENTS" is practically broken, and the line above "U.S. POSTAGE" is always significantly broken.

• Type II (#14) has a complete line above "U.S. POSTAGE." A significant part of the design is missing at the bottom, including most of both plumes and the line below "TEN CENTS."

• Type III (#15) has significant parts of both the top and bottom missing, including both the lines above "U.S. POSTAGE" and below "TEN CENTS."

• Type IV (#16) has the lines above "U.S. POSTAGE" and below "TEN CENTS" recut similarly to the one-cent 1851 stamp discussed earlier. This is the rarest ten-cent type, although the recut stamp is the most common one-cent type.

Like the one cent, the different types (and different Scott numbers) of the ten cent exist on the same sheet so that pairs (two stamps still attached together), strips (three or more attached stamps), and blocks (four or more stamps in two or more rows) showing more than one type can be found. When they are found, they are much desired by collectors and sell for far more than the total for both individual stamps. The ten-cent 1851 stamp is the

A proof of the ten cent 1851, and a used example of the same stamp.

easiest stamp in the 1851 set to find in good condition. The stamps were printed widely apart on the sheet, so that they are found with large margins. Additionally, because 10 cents represented a great deal of money in the 1850s, the stamps were usually well treated (even locked up!) before being placed on envelopes. Ironic as it may sound, many damaged stamps were probably damaged before they ever were placed on a letter. Some ten-cent stamps show severe damage, as they were the stamps used to pay postage to California and back. Often they were stuffed into some gold miner's pocket, or that of a covered-wagon traveler, for a lonely night around the campfire writing a letter home.

A proof of the 1851 twelve cent.

The Twelve Cent 1851 (#17)

The twelve-cent stamp pictures George Washington. This stamp was primarily used in pairs to pay the 24-cent overseas rate. For this reason, covers with pairs on them are not as valuable as covers bearing single stamps, a case of more being less. Twelve-cent stamps were printed very closely together; stamps with any margins, let alone clear margins, on all four sides are rare.

A large block of eleven of the twelve cent 1851. Multiples are avidly collected by specialists, and this piece is among the largest blocks known of the twelve cent. Rather than being worth eleven times the price of a single, it is worth more like 110.

A twelve cent 1851 tied on cover with a three cent 1851 to France.

THE 1857 ISSUE

Great Britain began perforating its general issue postage stamps some two years before the United States. In 1857, the Post Office Department contacted Toppan, Carpenter & Company (the printers of the stamps, and the surviving firm from Toppan, Carpenter, Casilear & Company, printers of the 1851 issue), and instructed them to begin planning to perforate the stamps. Ease of separation was cited as the reason, but it was also believed that perforated edges would make the stamps adhere better to the letters. Toppan, Carpenter & Company, with but four months left on the six-year contract they held to produce these stamps, was quite reluctant to go to all this additional expense with so little time remaining. A compromise was worked out whereby the government paid for the cost of the new perforating equipment, which would then become government property if the contract was not renewed. The perforation on the 1857s measures perf 15.

The One Cent 1857

The types of the perforated stamps are the same as those of the imperforate stamp. However, because new plates were prepared and used in addition to the original plate, Type I and IA, which are so very rare imperforate, are relatively more common on the perforated plate. This has led to some trickery, as certain collectors will trim the perforations off a #18 in an attempt to make it look like a #5. Fortunately, a dot in the circle around the portrait of Franklin at 8:00 was added to the later plate, making it impossible to fool knowledgeable philatelists.

And the original #5 has a characteristic *double transfer* (a doubling of the design due to faulty entry of the die onto the plate) not found on any of the perforated Type Is. Part way into the press run of the perforated stamps, a change was instituted. The stamps were aligned so closely together on the original plate that when perforations were placed between the stamps, they often cut far into the stamp design, and the post office complained.

We should realize that the printers of these stamps were not in fact aware that there were subtle differences in the stamps they were printing, and probably would not have cared very much if they had known. After all, they were under contract, with set delivery dates, to produce the postage stamps for a nation. The decisions that they made as to sheet size, spacing, and printing were purely utilitarian ones, dictated by concerns of cost and efficiency.

It is obvious, then, that when the one cent Type V was created, it was not done with the intent of confusing later philatelists. But as the perforations cut too far into the design, the post office objected, and when you are in business as Toppan, Carpenter was, and your client complains, you take steps to remedy the complaint. Accordingly, part of the design of the stamp was burnished (removed by scraping the steel on the plate) away on all sides, so that the stamp resembled Type III at the top, but is also missing quite a bit of design at the sides, which never happened in Type III. This is the Type V, known only on the perforated stamps.

Quality on the one cent 1857 perforated stamps is nearly always a problem. The entire 1857 issue is not graded as strictly as are the other United States stamps. There was simply no room to place the perforations except on part of the stamps, so collectors

must expect that even Very Fine or better specimens show portions of their designs with some perforation holes. The Type V (#24) is the exception to this rule—it was created solely to make more room, and spectacular examples are occasionally found. In ascending order of scarcity, this issue is listed #24, 20, 22, 23, 18, 21, 19, with the #19 approximately seventy-five times more scarce than the #24.

The three-cent 1857 stamp is the same as the three cent 1851 with the addition of perforations. While there are two types of three-cent 1851 stamps (#10 and #11), these two types are distinguishable by shade alone. The two types of the three-cent 1857 stamps are distinguished in that after perforating some of the

A one cent Type V—a pair in mint condition.

#11s, the frameline of the horizontal rows between the stamps were removed to make more room between the stamps for the perforation holes. Thus the Type I #25 has a frameline above and below the stamp, while the Type II #26 does not.

The #25 is about ten times more scarce than the #26. The #26 was the stamp that carried the bulk of the mail posted in this country during the years 1857 to 1861, and is the most common stamp in the 1857 series. In 1980, the stamp customarily traded at about the $1.50 level for an ordinary used example; unused versions began at about $30. Because of its relative accessibility, many collectors have specialized collections containing thousands of copies of this stamp. Often the stamp was found with what philatelists

A cover cancelled by the Chicago Supplementary mail cancellation. When a letter missed its connection with a ship because of late posting, the mailer had the option of using supplementary mail, whereby a faster tug took late-posted letters out to the departed ship. The fee was double the postage due on the letter, in this case 3 cents, and was payable in cash.

call a circular date stamp cancellation—a cancel containing the town name and the month and the day. Some collectors try to make what is called a "calendar collection"—a collection of 366 stamps cancelled for each day of the year. Theoretically, no date should be scarcer than any other except for February 29, of which there should be one-fourth as many. But completing a "calendar collection" usually requires searching through tens of thousands of stamps.

The years of this issue, 1857 to 1861, were an exciting era for America, and this is reflected philatelically. It was a period of western expansion, and collectors often seek cancellations from small western towns. The railroad was an active mail carrier, so collectors look for distinctive railway post office cancellations. So too, with steamboats on the Mississippi, gold and silver mines, and cavalry troops fighting the Indians—all of these bits of history produced letters, and all of them have distinctive cancellations known to and collected by philatelists.

And there was the Pony Express. Born in the hopes of rapid communication between the East and West Coast, the Pony Express riders set out from St. Joseph, Missouri, across Nebraska, over the Sierra Madres to California. Every 15 miles or so along the route a change station was built so that riders would always have fresh mounts. Here, horses were kept with the station master, and were saddled and made ready as the rider approached. The exchange of horses was a marvel of efficiency, with the rider hopping off one and onto another in a flash. Each rider traveled about 75 miles in a given ride, or about five or six exchanges, resting at the farthest exchange station before beginning a ride back.

The Pony Express could deliver a letter across the continent in ten days. But it was only in existence eighteen months, by which time the coincidence of the Civil War and the laying of the transcontinental telegraph forced this fascinating private post out of business.

A Pony Express cover, on a ten-cent government envelope, with a Pony Express stamp. The envelope is a patriotic design, used by the North as propaganda during the Civil War.

A proof of the five cent 1857. Note how the top and bottom projections were shaved off.

The Five- and Ten-Cent Stamps of 1857

The five cent 1857 is a very tricky stamp because its proper determination rests on both color and type factors. The types are relatively easy to distinguish, and they, too, were caused by the exigencies of the perforating machinery. In 1860, an engraver went back over the plate and cut off the tiny projectiles at the top and the bottom of the stamp, creating the second type; Type I still had the projectiles. The colors or shades of this stamp make it exceedingly difficult to distinguish the proper catalogue number, even for rather adept philatelists. The shades of Type I are brick red (#27), red brown (#28), Indian red (#28A), and brown (#29). The colors of the Type II are orange brown (#30) and

A rare example of the five cent printed on both sides. This is the reverse side. Most printed-on-both-side varieties were done intentionally, that is, the first print did not take properly and the printer turned the sheet over in an effort to save paper.

A fantastic cover used from Oregon City when Oregon was a territory, across the Atlantic to Ireland. Both transatlantic covers and territorials are extremely popular—to find them in a combination is a collector's dream.

brown (#30A). For the four colors of Type I, many philatelists have questioned the Scott catalogue listing of such minor distinctions—and they are indeed small differences. However, the Type II stamp creates no difficulties in identification as the orange brown and brown shades are very distinctive.

The ten cent 1857 is much like its earlier perforated counterpart, with the addition of a Type V, which is a cutaway plate leaving more room for the perforating machine. The ten cent 1857 comes in a multitude of shades, but unlike the five cent these are treated by collectors as the same stamps; only specialists attempt to find an example of each shade variety for their collection.

The twelve-cent (#36) stamp is just a perforated version of the earlier 1851 twelve cent. In late 1859, a new plate was prepared, which can be distinguished from the original plate by its light frameline instead of the usual heavy frameline around the stamp. A minor variety, Scott designates this #36b, and it sells for marginally more than the plate #1, #36.

The Twenty-Four-Cent, Thirty-Cent, and Ninety-Cent 1857 Stamps

All of the high denomination stamps of the 1857 issue are very rare. Only 750,000 of the 24-cent values were printed, although it is known that some were returned to the Post Office Department as unsold and then were destroyed. Experts estimate that perhaps 10,000 to 12,000 examples exist in collectors' hands. This estimate is one that meets with informal verification by those who peruse auction catalogues and dealers' stocks. Of the 30-cent value 337,000 were printed; again, some were returned unsold to the department. A fair evaluation of this stamp would be that between 8,000 to 10,000 survive. Of the 90-cent value 29,000 were issued, and some of these were returned to be destroyed. Because of the short period during which the 90-cent value was available before

A pair of the twelve cent perforated, imperforated between. This was accidentally issued and is considered an error.

A used example of the twenty-four cent, with freak perforations.

A proof example of the twenty-four cent 1857.

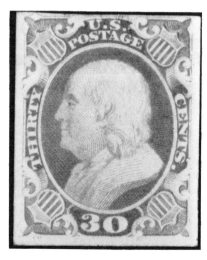

A proof example of the thirty cent 1857.

A proof example of the ninety cent 1857.

its demonetization, a somewhat higher percentage was saved, and experience indicates that there are perhaps 3,000 to 4,000 examples still in philatelic hands. After the Civil War, a number of the high values of the 1857 sets were retrieved from southern post offices and sold to stamp dealers.

It is worth remembering that over 24,000 copies of the five-dollar 1893 Columbus stamp were printed, out of which, because of its commemorative nature, its early popularity, and high face value, certainly 12,000 or more still survive. And yet a five-dollar

A genuinely used pair of the ninety cent on a piece. Such items are extremely difficult to prove genuine. On items of this type, more often than not, philatelists rely on what is called provenance; that is, the history of the item, when it was found, who has owned it and believed it to be genuine.

Columbian in reasonably nice condition, four times as common as the #39, sells for much much more. Popularity, you say. No doubt true, but popularity is influenced by availability. If a collector cannot find a stamp offered, as is often the case with the ninety cent 1857, he is very apt to replace it with something else on his want list.

DEMONETIZATION AND THE 1861s

Stamps monitor history; they are not issued in a vacuum. In its broadest sense, postal history is history. Throughout the early part of the nineteenth century great tensions between the North and the South, over economic matters and over slavery, culminated in the secession from the United States of the state of South Carolina on December 20, 1860, and of Mississippi, Florida, Alabama, Georgia, Louisiana, and Texas not long after. By February 4, 1861, the Confederate States of America had been organized and Jefferson Davis was elected President on February 9, 1861. As the North and South prepared for war, the North began to shut down the post offices in the South. The southern Postmaster General, John Reagan, encouraged the North in doing this, and

Cover marked "Southern Letter Unpaid"—indicating a southern use of a demonetized envelope.

instructed his postmasters to make their final accounts to the United States Post Office by April 30, 1861. Reagan specifically mentioned that all unsold stamps were to be returned and all monies owed to the North were to be paid. The South had hoped to be able to sever itself from the Union without conflict, and Reagan's order was issued as if the United States Post Office was a long-time contractor with whom the South would no longer be doing business. Many of the southern postmasters complied; but as his order was drafted in early April, before Sumter, the extent of the bitterness that was to arise between North and South was not foreseen. Because of this animosity, most postmasters from the South never made their final accounting with the United States Post Office, and some quantities of United States stamps were found in southern post offices after the war.

But the North never expected a proper accounting from the Confederate States. By June, the United States had ordered new stamps, and in August of 1861, a letter went out to the majority of northern post offices with new stamps, explaining that postmasters were to exchange the new stamps for any of the older ones that postal customers might bring in. All old stamps were to be returned so that they could be destroyed; thereafter they were demonetized, or shorn of their value. The North was afraid that the great mass of old stamps in the South would make their way back north, where they could be sold surreptitiously for hard currency to help the South finance the war. After late 1861, no stamps issued before 1861 had any postal validity at all. Even today, these stamps (#1–39) are still the only stamps issued by our government that are not recognized as postage. If you so desired, you could use any of the stamps of the valuable 1861 issue forward to post your letters.

THE 1861s

If this book were being written seventy years ago, we would speak of two 1861 issues, the Premier or August issue (for the month they supposedly came out, one month before the regular issue), and the Regular issue, which was issued in September of 1861. The Augusts, as they most usually were called, have very slight design differences from the issued stamps. It is now known beyond any reasonable doubt that they are not stamps at all, but rather essays submitted by the National Bank Note Company to the United States Post Office. As part of bids, companies were required to submit essays of what they proposed the new stamps should look like. Such a stipulation had been a requirement of contract bidding in the past, and the Post Office Department usually mandated rather significant changes in the designs of the stamps. But stamps were needed quickly now that the Civil War had started, and changes took time. With the most minor changes, the post office ordered the essays virtually as submitted.

The National Bank Note's essays (hereafter called the August issue as they are listed in the catalogue) have 1¢, 3¢, 5¢, 10¢, 12¢, 24¢, 30¢, and 90¢ values. All were printed on a very thin, hard, brittle paper. The paper damages easily, and for this reason many of the Augusts were damaged even though they were placed in philatelic hands from the earliest time. These stamps are listed in Scott as #55–62, with #58 being issued later to the public. When the #58 has been used, it is listed as #62B. With this sole exception, none of the other Augusts were generally issued to the public. With the exception of unused 3-cent and used 10-cent values, all of the Augusts are rare with less than a dozen sets existing. Though they were not originally postage stamps, they are listed that way in the catalogue and are great rarities.

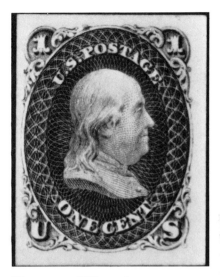

The one cent 1861 proof.

The real 1861 issue (#63–78) is the earliest United States set generally accessible to the philalelist. The stamps were issued between 1861 and 1866. Most of them sell used for under $20 to $25 each. The one-cent (#63) stamp is a beauty and was first issued, along with most of the rest of the set, about the middle of September. The two-cent (#73) stamp was not issued until July 1, 1863, and contains a large engraving of the face of Andrew Jackson. The stamp is black; philatelists refer to it as the "Blackjack." Two hundred and fifty million copies of this stamp were printed over its life, though well-centered examples are extremely rare—this may well be the most difficult United States stamp to find in well-centered condition. A perfectly centered two-cent Blackjack with large even margins sold years ago for 100 times the catalogue price, probably a record premium for quality alone.

The most spectacular double transfer known on an American stamp is found on the Blackjack. Called the Atherton Shift, it represents a complete doubling of the entire upper left corner. The stamp is worth several thousand dollars, against a catalogue value

A two-cent Blackjack proof.

A bisect of a Blackjack with a regular stamp used to pay the 3 cents first-class postage rate. The post office was probably out of one- and three-cent stamps.

A three-cent 1861 proof.

for the regular stamp of only a little more than $10. The Atherton Shift was no doubt discovered by the issuing authorities early and the plate was either repaired or destroyed; otherwise it would not be so very rare. As it is, only three or four copies are known. The shift has not received much publicity outside the Blackjack specialist circles and indeed, until very recently, was not even listed in the general catalogues. An example could be sitting, undiscovered, in the most ordinary collection.

The three cent 1861 is known in a myriad of shades. The earliest printings are printed in a truly striking red shade called Pink by the catalogues, but having a distinct tinge of blue in it. The Pinks (#64) are worth several hundred times the price of most of the other shades, which are much darker. If a panel of experts was asked to choose the one most common misidentification mistake made by novice, intermediate, and even advanced collectors, the overwhelming choice would be the confusion among the Pink (#64), the rose pink (#64b), and the reds (#65). All of the Pinks were printed with light-sensitive ink that darkens when exposed to light, destroying the variety. Besides hope springing eternal in the collector's breast, and the widespread philatelist's weakness for imagining his possessions to be more valuable than they really are, there is an additional factor at play here. For some reason that has never been addressed scientifically, the Pink's color is a hard one to memorize. When the shade is pointed out to them, novice collectors will make the distinctions with aplomb, sorting out large quantities of the stamp with unerring accuracy. But in a week's time, more often than not that same collector, if he has not worked on the stamp in the interim, will be back to making the same mistakes, confusing the shades and calling stamps Pink that do not even approach it. Several prominent collectors keep the several major shades of this stamp, including the Pink (#64), sorted and identified, and before they begin to work on quantities of the stamp, they review the shades again. Perhaps the human memory has a weakness over certain colors.

The common three-cent red of 1861 (#65) is a collector's dream. 1.75 billion copies of the stamp were issued. In quantity, the collector can buy them at under a quarter a piece. This is the most popularly collected specialized stamp in American philately, and one of the most fascinating ways to specialize in it is to collect "fancy cancellations." In the 1860s, the dictate came down from the postal authorities that each stamp on a letter had to be cancelled with a separate cancelling device that did not contain the town name and date. The town name and date, or circle date stamp (CDS), as philatelists call it, still had to be struck on the letter, but another cancellation had to be used as well to cancel the stamp. The reason given for this new postal regulation was that the CDS was usually indistinct when impressed upon a stamp, thus making an imperfect cancellation. A canceller that is used just to cancel the stamp is called a "killer," and it was up to the postmasters to provide these for themselves. The postmasters could cancel the stamps in any way they wanted. More imaginative postmasters carved their cancellers out of wood or cork; hearts, flowers, heads, or just about anything can be seen on these stamps. Fancy cancels began to die out about 1890 as the efficiencies of machine cancelling came in.

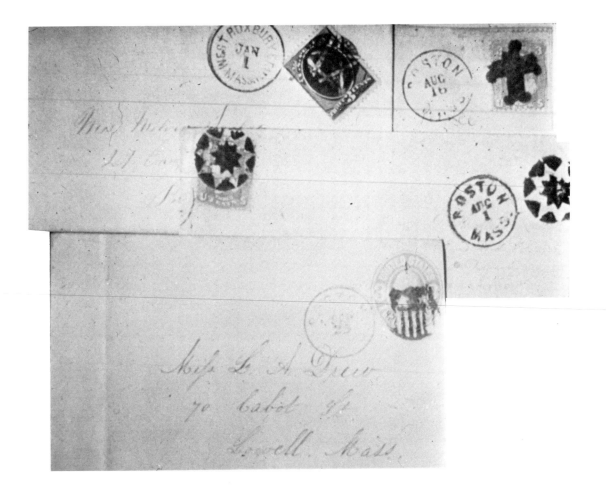

A group of covers with fancy cancels.

Brave in the Field—wise in
council—a true Patriot—Loyal
to the Constitution and Union.

A three cent 1857 used on a Patriotic cover.

Another fascinating area that is generally associated with the three cent 1861, though it is found with other stamps too, is that of "Patriotics." The year 1861 brought the outbreak of the Civil War. Just as patriotic Americans of this century have hung flags in their windows during wartime, envelopes bearing pro-Union designs were exceedingly popular in the North. There are hundreds of designs. Shades abound on the three cent 1861, and paper varieties are collected too. Many old-time philatelists report that the three cent 1861 is the last stamp "left." These old-timers were collecting when other early United States stamps were cheap enough to buy in quantity, before the great inflation that has driven up stamp prices since World War II. With the three cent 1861, a collector can still collect the way that collectors used to, where you can see and appreciate minute differences in shade and cancellation between hundreds of stamps that, until examined closely, look very much the same.

Encased postage. Due to a change shortage during the Civil War (there were hoarders then, too, as the price of metal went up), the government allowed private firms to encase postage in brass casings with their advertising on the reverse to be used as change.

The five-cent stamp comes in three shades, buff or olive brown (#67), red brown (#75), and brown (#76). The rarest of the three is the buff: it was printed on a very thin, brittle paper, which tends to crack almost spontaneously, making sound examples of this stamp quite rare. The postal authorities did not care for the color, which was deemed too light in shade and some thought it could be confused with the three cent. Late in 1861, only a short time after issue, it was replaced with the red brown. Of the buff 175,000 were issued, although probably just a few thousand still exist. The red brown (#75) and the brown (#76) are not scarce stamps: between the two, about 7.5 million were issued, 1 million of the #75 and 6.5 million of the #76. The red brown (#75) is a particularly delicious shade, and should not be confused with the ordinary shoe-polish brown of #76.

The ten-cent stamp issued in 1861 comes in two types. Type I has no line above "U.S. POSTAGE" while Type II does, although most experts use this telltale characteristic only as a second check. The Type I (#62B) is in a deep oak-leaf green shade that, with experience, proclaims its rare status. One half million #62B stamps were issued, though the stamp seems far scarcer than that. The regular Type II #68 is usually in a far lighter shade of green. Quantities issued of #68 are estimated at over 27 million, so this is not at all a rare stamp.

A real mess, but this cover was sent from Connecticut to an addressee in Paris. The 5 cents paid the American postage, so it was postage due in Paris. But the addressee had left. A friend, or perhaps a clerk at a hotel who had been left with money, put on the French stamps and forwarded the letter to Rome.

A ten cent Type I #62B.

Japan was opened to Western commerce in the mid-1850s, but the Japanese Postal System proved quite unable to handle transoceanic mail, as the island nation was just emerging from feudalism and had no merchant shipping to speak of. So the United States opened a post office in Japan. The #68, the ten cent Type II green, is the first stamp known to have been used from Japan, usually cancelled "Hiogo." Japanese Post Office cancellations are somewhat more common on the American 1867 and 1869 issues, reflecting increased trade between the two countries.

The twelve cent (#69) is a beautiful stamp, finely engraved like all of the 1861s. There are no varieties of any importance of this stamp. However, keep in mind that although most of the 1861s are not rare, they are exceedingly difficult to find in Very Fine or better condition. As a rule, they were perforated poorly, with the perforations customarily cutting into the design. Stamps centered so poorly that only two-thirds of the design shows are not rare. Too, the choice of paper was poor, being very brittle. Add to this the early "stamp saver's" penchant for peeling stamps off envelopes with a knife (it did not matter 100 years ago if a stamp was thinned), and it's easy to see why fewer than one copy in 100 of the 1861s remain in choice condition.

A ten cent Type II #68. Note the line over "U.S. POSTAGE."

Three different stamps with Japanese cancellations used from the United States postal agency in Japan. All are cancelled "Hiogo," all are rare; but the single frameline cancellation (at left) is far scarcer than the other two.

A proof of the 1861 twelve cent.

A proof of the 1861 twenty-four cent.

A proof of the 1861 ninety cent.

The balance of the set, the twenty-four cent (#70 and #78, depending on shade), the thirty cent (#71), and the ninety cent (#72), are all scarce but not rare stamps that are exceedingly difficult to find in appealing condition. The ninety cent (#72) has been a real star in terms of investment performance in the last few years—representing, of course, the discovery of its rarity, not the increase of its rarity itself. Off-cover used examples can be found; mint copies are rarities; and examples genuinely used on cover, of which only a few exist, have shot up in value from about $10,000 each to well over $50,000 in just a few years.

THE GRILLS (1867 ISSUE)

The postal authorities of the United States had a paranoic streak about postal users soaking stamps off envelopes, cleaning off the cancellations, and reusing the stamps. Philatelists who have examined millions of stamps and covers of the period know that this was pure fantasy on the part of the Post Office Department. The hard evidence does not support the theory that cleaning and reusing stamps was a problem of any magnitude whatsoever. Be that as it may, when a customer the size of the Post Office Department tells its printer to look for a way to make such cleaning impossible, the printer usually will find one.

Several schemes were advanced to solve this "problem." One idea, called patent cancels, was to use a canceller that cut the stamp, as well as cancelling it with ink, rendering its reuse unlikely. One small factor, however, was not taken into account: when you cut a stamp on a letter, you cut the letter as well. Postal patrons, who have always complained about the speed of delivery and the condition in which their letters arrived, reacted unenthusiastically when this plan was tried.

Another innovation was to print stamps on a paper that was made by gluing two layers of paper together—a thick bottom layer and a very thin top layer. This was called double paper. In theory, when such a paper was soaked off an envelope, the paper would separate and the top layer on which the stamp was printed would be so thin that the stamp printing would disintegrate. That was the theory! In practice, as often as not, the paper did not separate when soaked because it was glued too well. And sometimes, especially on hot, humid days, the stamp would separate spontaneously. Though philatelists know double paper was tried, especially on the later Bank Note issues, we don't know how widespread its use was.

Other countries were concerned with philatelic reuse too. The solution effected by Great Britain was to print its stamps on what is called *chalky* paper, a heavily coated paper that does not allow the ink to seep deeply into the paper fibers. When soaked off an envelope, the design would often mottle, or spread, and when chemical ink eradicators were used, the stamps would lose their design entirely. Other countries, notably the Dutch Indies, would print some of their stamps in what are called *fugitive inks*—inks that only lay on the surface of the paper. It is always a treat to see a novice collector's face when he drops several of these stamps in water to soak and they come out bare and white.

But the United States wanted to keep all of its stamps engraved, and the Great Britain and Dutch Indies answers were not compatible with line engraving. After turning down a brainstorm that would have put a small amount of gunpowder in the stamp paper during the printing process to be detonated by hitting the stamp with the postmark (never, to the Post Office Department's credit, seriously considered), a man named Charles Steel came up with a plan for a machine that grills.

A grilling machine has tiny pyramids that make minute cuts through the paper, after printing and gumming—the theory being that with the paper cut, the cancelling ink will seep deeper in, rendering it impossible to clean all evidence of the cancel away. And the little cuts are truly small: most grills cover less than half the stamp and have over 200 tiny cuts. The grills were applied to all of the stamps of the 1861 issue, creating the 1867 issue, and they would not be particularly interesting were it not for the fact that being a new process, there was a good deal of trial and error to see what worked. Grill types are referred to by letter (A to L and Z), though only A to F and Z are important to distinguish. A little trick that will aid you in seeing the grill better is to place the stamp face down in a watermark tray and add a bit of watermark fluid. The grill shows up darkly in the tray for the simple reason that where the grill breaks the paper, the paper is thinner. Some philatelists use tracing paper and artist's graphite to measure the grill. They place the stamp face down on a hard surface, place the paper over the stamp, and rub on the graphite. The grill usually shows up well, though this is a cumbersome business. With practice, most grills are easy to see unaided and to identify properly with the use of the tray.

Grills with Points Up (A, B, and C)

The "A" grill is the easiest grill of all to identify as it is the only one that extends over the entire stamp. It was the first grill issued, and it didn't work out very well. The large amount of grilling weakened the paper and made the stamp difficult to separate neatly along the perforations. When users tried to separate the stamps, they were frequently torn. The three cent (#79) is the most common of the three stamps known with an A grill; the quantity estimated issued is 50,000. Experience indicates that only 2,000 still remain in collectors' hands. Undamaged, well-centered copies are practically unknown. The five cent A grill (#80) is a great rarity; less than 2,000 were issued, and only four or five can currently be accounted for. No unused copies are known. If you wish to acquire this stamp, you would be wise to buy the first example that you see; only one example generally is sold during any generation. The same is true for the thirty cent (#81), with again only six examples known, all defective and all selling for over $100,000.

The B grill, like the A and the C, has the grill point facing up.

Grilled all over, with a fancy "U.S." killer cancellation as a bonus. The "grilled all over" is a rare stamp, and because the perforations so weakened the paper, it is almost always found damaged.

This means that the cutting pyramids of the grill machine were placed to do their work at the back of the stamp. The grill measures 18 by 15 millimeters, rather large by grill standards; or, when expressed in grill points or rows, which most collectors prefer, twenty-two rows by eighteen rows. Only one cover bearing four stamps was known with the B grill, and it is the 3-cent value (#82). The stamps have been taken off the cover. The C grill measures 13 by 16 millimeters, or sixteen to seventeen rows by eighteen to twenty-one rows. It is known only on the three cent (#83), and although rare, this is a stamp every collector can hope to attain. Three hundred thousand were estimated issued, so that though scarce, they are more abundant than their other "Points Up" brethren. The "Points Up" grill was for the most part unsuccessful. Placing the grill so that it pushed and cut up visibly disfigured the stamp. It was not long before placing the grill points down was tried. This process still produced the same amount of protection against cleaning while not greatly affecting the appearance of the stamps.

Grills with Points Down (D, E, F, and Z)

The D grill measures 12 by 14 millimeters, or fifteen rows or points by seventeen to eighteen rows (the reason that the number of rows sometimes varies within a grill is that they were set only approximately on the grilling machine, so there are slight differences). It is known on two stamps, the two-cent Blackjack (#84) and the three cent (#85). The numbers issued are 200,000 and 500,000 respectively, so that a fair evaluation of the number surviving in collectable condition would be perhaps between 2,000 and 5,000 of each.

The E grill is the second most common grill, measuring eleven by thirteen millimeters (or fourteen by fifteen to seventeen points), and is found on the one cent (#86), two cent (#87), three cent (#88), ten cent (#89), twelve cent (#90), and fifteen cent (#91). Though all E grills are scarcer than the stamps without grill (the 1861 issue), they are not rare. The F grill is the most common of all. It is found on the one cent (#92), two cent (#93), three cent (#94), five cent (#95), ten cent (#96), twelve cent (#97), fifteen cent (#98), twenty-four cent (#99), thirty cent (#100), and ninety cent (#101). This is a very narrow grill, measuring nine millimeters by fourteen millimeters (or eleven to twelve by fifteen to seventeen points), which was the grill the printers finally settled on. Scarcer too than the 1861 issue without grill, none of these stamps rates as rare either.

The rare grill with points down is the Z grill—which is also the most difficult grill to identify. The size of the grill is virtually identical to the E grill. However, the tiny cuts that each pyramid grill cutter makes on the Z grill are horizontal cuts (cuts going across the stamp) whereas on all other grills these cuts are vertical. While this is a small difference, it is a significant one. The Z grill is generally very rare. There are only three copies known of the one cent with Z grill (#85A). However, due to most collectors' unfamiliarity with grills, more (though certainly not many more) may be discovered. The two cent with the Z grill (#85B) is the one stamp in the Z grill family that most collectors can aspire to. The number issued is estimated at 100,000; probably a few thousand still exist in collectable condition, so it is something of a bargain at its current price of only a few hundred dollars. The three cent Z grill (#85C) is a rare stamp. The ten cent (#85D) is a rarity of the magnitude of the one cent, with only a handful known. The twelve cent (#85E) is not rare, though the fifteen cent (#85F) is another rarity.

The Z grills amply illustrate the problem that philately has with grills. They are difficult to identify and for this reason are overlooked by most philatelists. Because of their relative unpopularity, rare grills attain nowhere near the high prices that they would achieve if they were "face different" varieties. Many collectors ignore the grills entirely. The two cent Z grill (#85B), which would sell for thousands of dollars if it were a commemorative, only sells for hundreds. Buyers must beware of forged grills, as well. It is not very difficult to attempt to forge a grill on the back of a stamp and to turn a five-dollar variety into an apparent $5,000 one. But such work is rarely convincing to anyone even slightly familiar with grills, though collectors should insist on appropriate authentication or certification on expensive items and would be wise to consult the experts. This is especially true if the item is offered at a "bargain basement" price; it was usually made there.

As an aside, Lester Brookman, one of the greatest experts on United States stamps, believed that there were two main types of collectors: those who suspect that nothing is counterfeit and those who suspect that everything is counterfeit. What he meant is that unknowledgeable collectors (and, increasingly, investors) have no idea how easy it is to create a variety that can look convincing to someone who has never seen it before. At the same time, a little knowledge can make some collectors so skeptical that they never purchase any stamps for their collection. American philatelists are fortunate. Because of firm anticounterfeiting laws, nearly all of the forgeries and alterations of United States stamps are tawdry affairs made quickly before the Feds closed in. Knowledgeable experts can tell the grills and any other variety with absolute certainty.

The complete set of 1869s, to the thirty cent, in proofs.

THE 1869 ISSUE

The 1869 issue of the United States was the world's first pictorial stamp. Until that time all United States postage stamps, and all world postage stamps for that matter, depicted either heads of states or numerical figures. The 1869 issue was unpopular from the start. But it is important to note that deriding the quality and subject matter of United States stamps has long been an American pastime.

The one-cent buff (#112), with Benjamin Franklin's picture, evoked praise for its execution but great criticism for its color, which is a dull buff. The color did not show the detail very well and in its lightest shades is very difficult even to see. The two cent, in brown (#113), is a beautiful stamp that shows a man riding a horse. Equestrians from the beginning said that the designer of the stamp could never have ridden horses, and that no self-respecting horse would be caught with its legs in that position. The *New York Herald* said the scene looked like "[John Wilkes] Booth's death ride into Maryland." The beautiful three cent (#114) shows a locomotive, and is printed in an ultramarine shade that makes lovely copies rare. The six cent (#115) shows General Washington, and the ten cent (#116) in orange is exceedingly difficult to find in excellent condition. The twelve cent (#117) shows the ship *Adriatic*.

The high values of the 1869s begin with the fifteen cent. This was the first American stamp to be printed in two colors. Two-color printing using the line-engraved printing method is not easy.

The stamps must be printed in two runs through the press, aligning the two colors, in this case making sure the vignette (or center) is balanced within the frame. Such centering of the printing is almost never perfect; the vignette always is off center in one direction or another. Surprisingly enough, stamp collectors who will drag a stamp's price down for virtually any reason, real or imagined, do not pay attention to the centering of the vignette in a two-colored line-engraved stamp.

This fifteen-cent stamp shows a pictorial representation of the landing of Columbus. There are two types of the stamp, one (#119) with the center vignette framed by a line and a small diamond at the top (below the T of "POSTAGE"), and another unframed (#118). The stamp was originally printed without the diamond and it is about twice as scarce that way. After a short while, the stamp department of the post office thought it would look better if the diamond took up what was considered to be an

An invert of the 1869 fifteen cent.

excess of white space around the vignette, and this small change was made. The stamp with the diamond is known inverted—caused, of course, when one of the passes through the press was done improperly and the paper was turned around after one color had been printed and before the next. Then, as now, there were inspectors, but inspectors do not always catch everything they are supposed to. In philately, their mistakes make the hobby more interesting. It is odd, of course, that collectors value inverts so highly. Businessmen routinely throw away inverted letterheads, as do people who get an imperfect pad of checks from their bank. In stamps, such things are rarities. Though inverts are always called *inverted centers,* in some cases (like this one), they are really inverted frames. It depends on which was printed first, the vignette or the frame, and in the case of this stamp, the vignette was printed first. Only a few fifteen-cent inverts exist and they sell for thousands.

An invert of the twenty-four cent. Most of the known inverts are very poorly centered.

The twenty-four cent 1869 (#120) has been acclaimed by many enthusiasts, the authors included, as the finest stamp ever produced by any nation. The colors are green frame, violet vignette. The vignette measures 3/8 inch wide by 3/16 inch high, and the engraver has portrayed a faithful reproduction of John Trumbull's *Declaration of Independence*. With a magnifying glass, an observer can identify the six principal figures in this stamp by the features alone, which is rather astonishing when you figure that each head is smaller than the head of a pin. This stamp is the pinnacle of the engraver's art, even though he was not helped by the color choice as the violet center sometimes begins to fade. The stamp is known with an "inverted center"—again, really an inverted vignette. Probably less than twenty of the twenty-four-cent inverts exist, including a block of four.

The thirty cent (#121) is not very uncommon used, but it is a very rare stamp on cover. High denominations, such as the thirty cent, were generally used on packages or on very heavy large-sized envelopes—not the type of items that are often saved. An invert of this stamp is known, too, though this one was not "discovered" until years after the stamp was issued. This is because the bland colors of the stamp, combined with generally heavy cancellations and the invert's intrinsic rarity, kept its existence hidden for almost thirty years. It always pays to look carefully at your stamps. In all, about twenty copies of the invert have been found; more probably exist.

The ninety cent (#122) is a beautiful stamp, so lovely that it is hard to believe that postal users found this stamp, like the other 1869s, ugly. The stamp is very rare, and it is the only regular two-color variety of the 1869s that never accidentally came out inverted. It did so intentionally! That's right. The government issued proofs of the fifteen cent, twenty-four cent, thirty cent, and ninety cent with inverted centers. But the inverted proofs, of which only 100 were issued, were printed on thick card stock similar to shirt cardboard, though of finer quality, and were issued imperforated.

Part of the reason for the unpopularity of this set was its new size, which most postal users felt was far too small. The stamps are about two-thirds the size of those that they replaced. The colors chosen were considered too dull and bland, but this extreme criticism strikes modern philatelists as odd. To our eyes, the 1869s are among the most beautiful stamps the United States has ever

An invert of the thirty cent.

*One of the largest known blocks
of the thirty cent.*

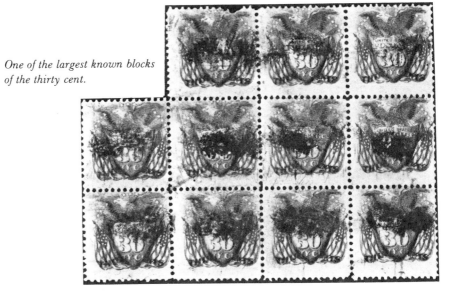

The ninety cent 1869 in proof.

produced. The small size that the 1869 postal users disparaged we find appealing in its simplicity and innovativeness. The colors that were ridiculed have held up quite well over the years, so that, on balance, the 1869s look far fresher and brighter than many stamps that seemed so much better printed then. To people in the nineteenth century the choice of designs seemed radical, and to have illustrated scenes rather than heads of state appeared insolent. Now, however, we are accustomed to so many cluttered commemoratives that the 1869s make a refreshing change. But the critics won the day, and the set was withdrawn in 1870 after less than a year of duty.

THE BANK NOTES

Beginning with 1870 and the issues that philatelists term the Bank Notes, United States stamps entered a new philatelic period. These stamps are called the Bank Notes because they were printed over their twenty-year span by three successive bank note-printing companies, the National, the Continental, and the American Bank Note companies.

The different printings of these stamps by the three companies are treated by philatelists as different stamps. For years, some collectors have had difficulty identifying among the printings, but in recent years the trouble has been alleviated. Our knowledge of these stamps has increased, but the reason that the stamps are easier to distinguish is primarily because the differences between the stamps are now better explained. For years philatelic writers wrote only for a specialized audience; only in the last twenty years have easier explanations in plain English been available. The lower values of the stamps can be distinguished with little experience; the higher values are more difficult.

There are four different sets of Bank Notes. The first set is #134–144, printed by the National Bank Note Company on grilled paper. Next are #145–155, printed by the National Bank Note Company on ungrilled paper.

It should be remembered that the grills on the grilled Bank Notes were placed in a perfunctory manner. The government maintained its order that all supplied stamps were to be grilled, but beyond that they rarely inspected the stamps very carefully. They were beginning to tire of the idea of grilling stamps, and within a few months the National Bank Note Company was permitted to supply stamps with no grill at all. Further, the grills on the stamps that they did supply grilled were rarely fully impressed, and often had the appearance of several sheets having been placed in the grilling machine at once.

After the ungrilled National Bank Note Company's printing of the issue called the Bank Notes come #156–166, printed by the Continental Bank Note Company, who outbid the National for the new contract that was awarded in 1873. The Continental added small distinguishing marks to the stamp plates so that they could tell their own printed stamps from those printed by National. These distinguishing marks are called by philatelists "secret marks" and the general stamp catalogues illustrate them quite well. The secret marks do not exist on the high values of the set, which must be told by shade alone.

Finally, there is the American Bank Note printing of #182–191, printed in 1879 on the same plates but on a soft porous paper. Soft porous paper is extremely distinctive. When held to the light, the paper shows a marked weave; when bent, it bends very easily, with none of the spring of the earlier papers. But the most distinctive test is to place a stamp face down in a watermark tray filled with watermark fluid. There, the distinctive weave will invariably proclaim its status. The American Bank Note Company printed stamps from these plates for years, and late in the 1880s retouched some of the designs. These are given special catalogue numbers and the subtle differences are well illustrated in the catalogue.

The complete set of Bank Notes in proofs.

Since the Bank Notes were the postage stamps for a nation for so long a period, hundreds of printings were necessary. Of the three-cent stamp, 6.5 billion stamps were printed and sold over a twenty-year period. Collectors avidly specialize in these stamps. Indeed, with the exception of the grilled Bank Notes and the higher values above the twenty-four cent, used Bank Notes are quite common and well within the price range of most collectors.

A pair of the three cent. It is shown here upside down to emphasize the fancy cancellation, which is the man's head in a circle.

An appealing block of the ninety-cent Bank Note.

Bank Notes can be collected in basically two ways. First, a collector can attempt to own one of each of the stamps printed by each of the printing companies. This is how most collectors attempt it, and this is how the stamps are arranged in most catalogues and albums. The second method is gaining more and more favor. It begins with finding one of the low-value stamps that you especially like and creating a specialized collection. For about $100, a collector can purchase well over 2,000 of the three-cent Bank Notes. Each stamp is a piece of history in its own shade and with its own distinct cancellation. Specializing like this is usually an adjunct to a general United States collection and can offer satisfactions all its own.

The higher-value Bank Notes have great interest because of their rarity and the problems in finding them in excellent condition. The twenty-four cent is an exceedingly difficult stamp. The color has faded badly to such a dull shade of light lilac (listed as purple in the catalogue but not what people would usually call purple) that often the details are difficult to see. The twenty-four cent National grill is one of America's rarest stamps: only 2,000 were printed and probably but a handful remain. If it were a face different variety, rather than a variety with a grill (always less popular with collectors), it would no doubt sell for five or ten times its current $10,000 price tag. The twenty-four cent is known in only two ways—grilled and ungrilled, both printed by the National Bank Note Company. It is a matter of record that the Continental Bank Note Company printed and issued twenty-four-cent stamps in 1873, but these stamps are indistinguishable from the National printings.

For years these twenty-four-cent Continentals were listed as Scott #165, at about the same price as #153; but because the two varieties are identical, wisdom overcame tradition, finally, and the listing was taken out. There is an old story about a stamp dealer, back in the days when these two identical ungrilled twenty-four-cent stamps were given separate catalogue listings, who kept all his twenty-four-cent Bank Notes in his stock book, with no number on them, of course. When asked for one or the other, he would pull two examples out of the book, and begin discoursing on their differences and why one was the variety for which the collector was looking. There was far less substance than salesmanship in all of this, though because both stamps sold for the same price, advantage was taken only of the truth.

Another block of the ninety-cent Bank Note. The imprint reads "National Bank Note Company"; they made the plates, but the stamps were printed by any of three different companies.

REISSUES AND SPECIAL PRINTINGS

Many of the most precious varieties of United States stamps were not regularly issued to the public. In 1875, the United States Postal Department wished to have on sale at the Centennial Post Office, which was to be at the Centennial celebration in Philadelphia, examples of all United States stamps that had been issued to that time. This was a public relations ploy on the part of a department proud of its stamps that also wanted specimens to sell to the public. Anyone who so desired was permitted to buy them, but because stamp collecting was in its infancy, few people availed themselves of this spectacular offer. The stamps were printed on different paper from the originals and in slightly different colors, so that an entire new category of stamps was created. All the reissues are rare and all are expensive.

For years, the controversy has raged over just how valid the reissues are. After all, they were sold more for souvenir than for postal purposes, even though they could be used on letters. But for the last fifty years or so the dispute has died down, and the reissues now grace many fine collections.

The reissues of the first two stamps that were made for the 1875 Centennial are not reissues at all. The Post Office Department believed that the original dies for the first two stamps (#1 and #2) had been destroyed in 1851. New dies were prepared, so these stamps are much more accurately designated as reproductions than reissues. They were printed in sheets of fifty, imperforate and ungummed. Forty-seven hundred of the five-cent reproduction (#3) and 3,800 of the ten-cent reporduction (#4) were printed.

The reissues of the 1857s are great rarities. The one cent #40 is the most common of the set, with 3,846 issued. This stamp is the perfect Type I, with all portions of the design complete. The shades of all of the reissues are quite different from the original stamps though, so there is no danger of collectors being fooled and purchasing a rare reissue as an even rarer mint Type I or 1857. Of the balance of the set, #41–47, the largest number of any value printed and sold is under 500, and they all sell for $2,000 each. It is situations like this that attract speculators to stamps. They see a very popular collectable that is extremely rare selling for a comparatively low price—one could control all of the available supply of the reissues for a relatively small amount of money.

For a long time, stamp economists have been attempting to

The originals of the 1847 issue, U.S. #1 and #2.

explain the relatively low price of stamps like the 1857 reissue. Several reasons have been put forward. First, they were not new designs, so there is a certain amount of collector resistance to paying large sums of money for a stamp that looks pretty much like one that they already have. Second, most collectors collect in inverse chronological fashion, starting with the present and working their way backward. There are, unfortunately, too few collectors with the means and inclination to work back into the nineteenth century. And if they do, they are most concerned with getting face different specimens. These explanations are fine, but they miss a more poignant aspect of philately and philatelic prices. These stamps, and other reissues like them, are so scarce that no

An 1875 reproduction of the five cent 1847.

An 1875 reproduction of the ten cent 1847. Compare with the original (page 128) noting the subtle differences, especially in the eyes.

more than a dozen or so of each are traded in any given year. Philatelists base their wants on what they see, and reissues are not offered often enough to whet the palate of most collectors. In fact, some are almost never publicly offered, with prominent dealers having these rarities on innumerable want lists so that they sell as soon as they come to the market. Thus the reissues go to the serious collector with patience and a penchant for completion; but the casual monied collector or investor passes over them, primarily because he never sees them. Accordingly, the upward price pressure is lessened.

Of the 1861 reissue, again the entire set was reissued on a white paper in slightly different colors. Just over 300 complete sets were

The one-cent 1857 reissue.

The five-cent 1857 reissue.

The twelve-cent 1857 reissue.

The twenty-four-cent 1857 reissue.

The thirty-cent Bank Note reissue.

The two-cent Bank Note Special Printing. Note how, despite the perforations, the stamp appears to be cut from the sheet with scissors. This is characteristic of all Bank Note Special Printings.

sold. The 1869 reissues are more common; perhaps the short time they were on sale as regular issues encouraged patrons at the Centennial Exposition to buy examples of an issue that they hardly remembered. Still, only 1,350 sets were sold. The balance of the stamps on sale at the Centennial Exposition are called special printings, as the stamps of which they are examples were currently on sale at the post offices. The special printings are in slightly different shapes from the originals, and slightly fresher in appearance; but, unlike the reissues, they are exceedingly difficult to tell from the original issued stamps.

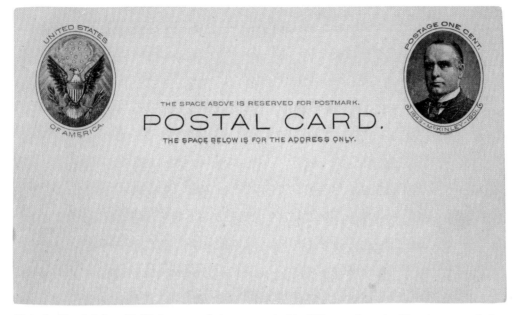

Plate 1. The full-face McKinley, one of the most valuable U.S. postal cards. The story goes that McKinley's widow so disliked his portrait on this card that the post office decided not to issue them. A box of 500 somehow were circulated, most of which became printed with the return address of its user, a garbage scow contractor in New York.

Plate 2. Perhaps the most valuable cover in the world: two four-margined examples of the One Penny Post Office Mauritius. This item will sell next for well over $1,000,000.

Plate 3. Two of the rare early issues of Switzerland.

Plate 4. A great rarity of aerophilately—a cover carried by Charles Lindbergh on his first transatlantic crossing.

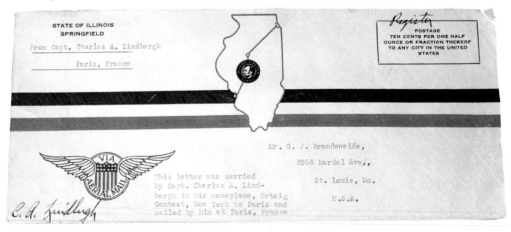

Plate 5. The 3-skilling error of color on the first stamp of Sweden. This stamp is unique, though its price has been affected in recent years by suspicions that its yellow color might be a changeling from its supposed color, green.

Plate 6. The first issue of Brazil, called by philatelists the "Bull's Eyes" because the design resembles the eye of a bull. This strip of three contains two 30-reis values and a 60-reis value. Such se-tenant combinations are exceedingly rare.

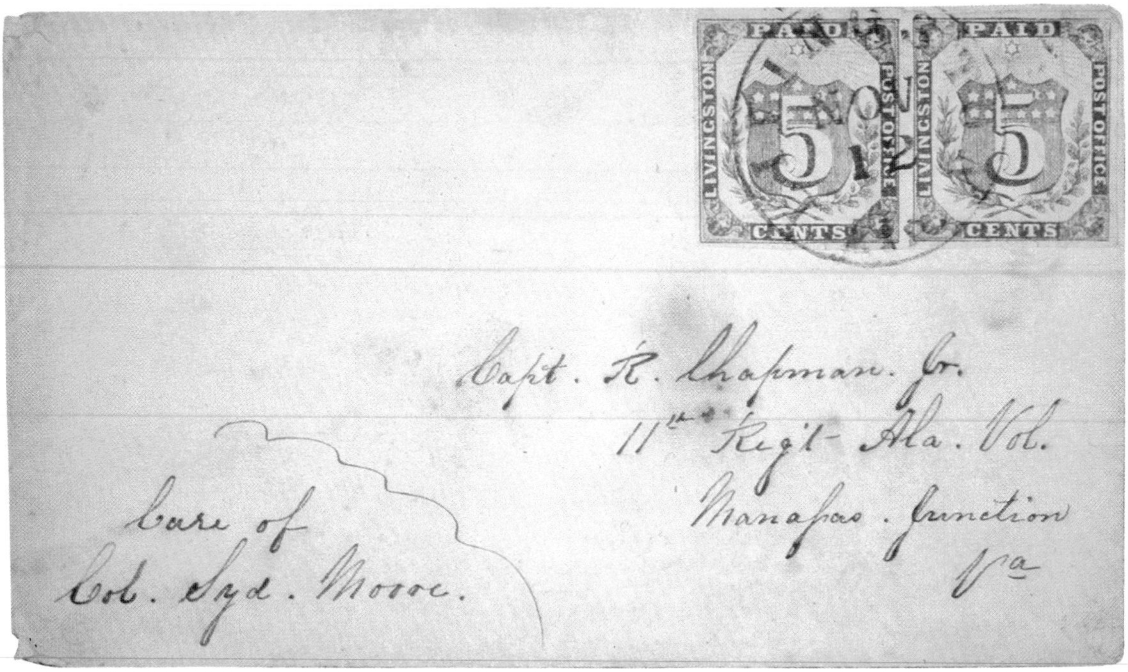

Plate 7. One of the rarest Confederate State covers, from Livingston, Alabama.

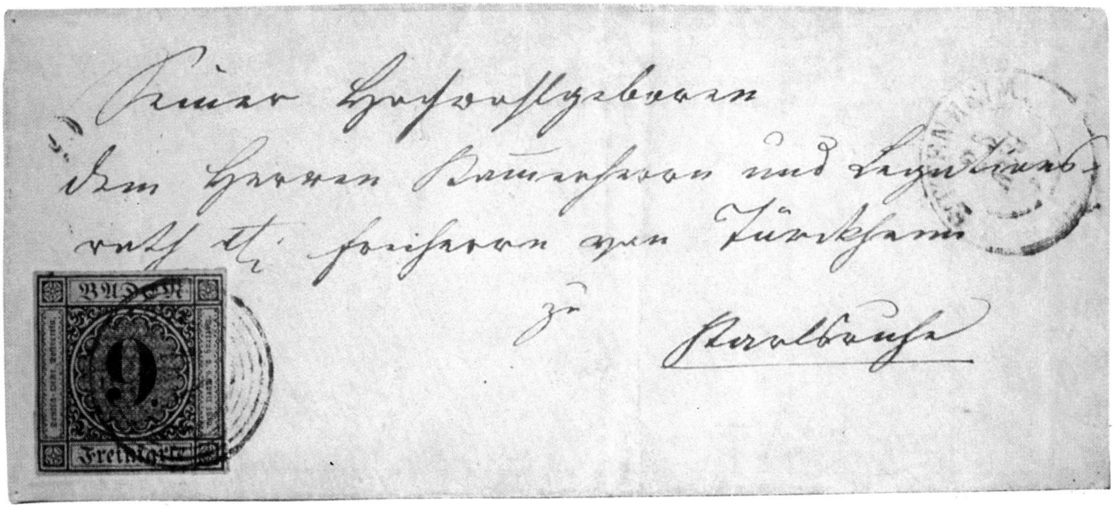

Plate 8. This stamp was supposed to be printed on rose paper rather than green (the green was for the 6-Kreutzer value, not the 9), but somebody made an error, and today it would cost $150,000 to buy this cover.

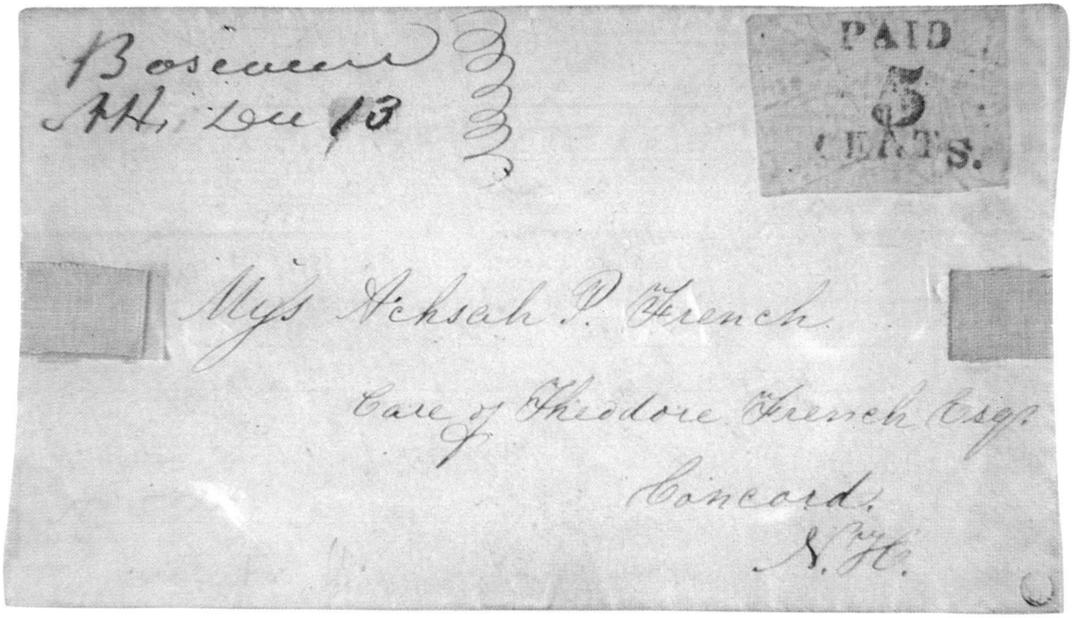

Plate 9. Before the United States issued stamps, individual postmasters were permitted to issue their own stamps. The postmaster of Boscawen, New Hampshire, did so; only one has survived.

Plate 10. A block of four of the two-cent Pan American invert.

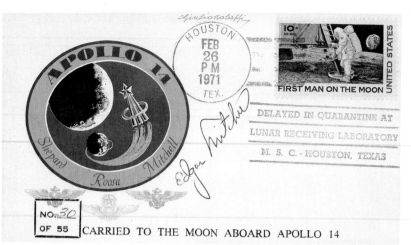

Plate 11. A modern rarity. This cover went to the moon.

Plate 12. A block of twenty of the one-cent Pan American invert.

Plate 13. A pair of the first issue of Saxony on cover. From the first, Saxony #1 was a rarity and no less than twenty different counterfeits exist, most made to be sold as space fillers. This cover is genuine and sells for over $100,000.

Miss Eliza A. Dawson

Carl Jacob H. Dawson

273 Cherry Street

New York

Oct 4. (probably 1852)

Plate 14. The rarest Hawaii cover, with a two-cent and five-cent Missionary, along with two three-cent United States stamps to pay the postage once it reached the States. A great rarity.

Plate 15. The rare one-cent "Z" grill.

Plate 16. Four different proposals submitted to the British government during the Treasury Competition of 1839. If any of these had won, they would have set the standards by which all stamps are judged.

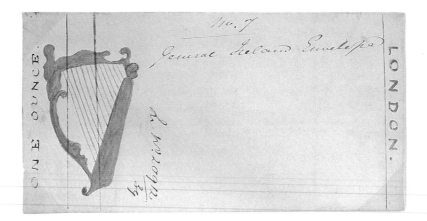

The three-cent Special Printing.

The fifteen-cent Special Printing.

The seven-cent Special Printing.

MODERN UNITED STATES PHILATELY

After 1890, United States stamps changed. For the first forty-three years of stamps, printing methods were not nearly as mechanized, resulting in numerous printing varieties. Furthermore, the wide variety of cancellations on the stamps and the panorama of different usages in the earlier period encourage collectors to specialize in a particular issue or even a particular stamp. From the 1890 philatelic period onward, this highly specialized collecting of a single issue or even a single stamp has been done far less commonly. There are comparatively few varieties in post-1890 stamps. Color was matched with precision, resulting in few of the color variations between printings so common in the earlier period. The economics of automatic cancelling equipment forced a sameness into American cancellations of the modern period that has tended to discourage cancellation collectors. And the rising popularity of philately after 1890 has meant that quantities of philatelic material were saved, resulting in fewer real rarities. In addition, the goal of discovering the usage and varieties of each stamp, which is one of the joys of philately, was no longer necessary. Contemporary philatelists in the post-1890 period were there to chronicle each variety first hand. When you add to all of this the United States Post Office Department's catering to collectors in an attempt to improve its own balance sheet, the picture of the modern philatelic era is complete.

But don't for a minute think that post-1890 philately is boring; it is not, it is just more predictable. And because early philatelists saved quantities of post-1890 issues, don't think that the prices will be low. The period from 1890 to 1930 is the most popular philatelic period among intermediate and expert collectors, so while more material is available, more collectors are competing for it as well.

A complete set of proofs of the 1890 set.

An imperf pair of the ninety cent of the 1890 issues.

1890 Issues

The 1890 issues (#219–229) are attractively printed. Although not uncommon in used condition, Very Fine mint copies are very scarce. Each of the values is known imperforate. The imperforates were deliberately ordered by the Post Office Department when it turned over its entire collection to the National Postal Museum (which still operates today under the name Postal History Division of the History and Technology Museum of the Smithsonian). When the collection was turned over, a number of gaps were discovered in the collection, especially in stamps such as inverts that were inadvertently produced and were never ordered by the department. The museum used the imperforate 1890 issue to trade with dealers and collectors for stamps that the collection needed. Congress did not appropriate money to expand the collection, no doubt feeling that philatelists were no great lobby to contend with. But because of the museum's trades, such items as the fifteen-cent, twenty-four-cent, and thirty-cent 1869 inverts can be seen today by people who otherwise would never have the opportunity. Considering their rarity, the imperforate pairs do not sell for a great deal, probably attesting to some distaste over the fact that these imperforates were manufactured deliberately by the government to trade at a premium over their face.

The Columbians

Perhaps the most popular United States series is the 1893 Columbian Exposition issue. In its day, the set was a hotly debated boondoggle, causing protests from philatelists around the world. It helped create the organization of the Society for the Suppression of Spurious Stamps (or SSSS, as they called themselves). And it

A complete set of the 1893 Columbian Exposition issue in proofs.

caused the post office no end of joy at the profits it reaped. Such post office profiteering was quite conscious. In their memos to one another, it was apparent that the postal officials designed the set so that sales of the stamps to collectors would increase Post Office Department revenues.

The occasion of the issue was the 400-year anniversary celebration of Columbus's discovery of the New World—a celebration held, somewhat belatedly, in Chicago in 1893. The Columbians, as philatelists refer to the set, were the world's first commemorative stamps. Commemoratives are special event stamps issued to draw attention to an event. Such commemoratives are quite popular today, with some thirty or more issued annually.

Being a new series, actively promoted by the government, and having so very many high-valued stamps, the Columbians were speculated in heavily right from the start. To a very real extent, this set can be said to be the first to attract investors. And they got walloped! Following what seems to be the unwritten lemming rule of most stamp speculators, hundreds of collectors put away thousands of these Columbian stamps, far more than the tiny stamp market of the 1890s could accommodate. For over twenty-five years after their issue, dollar-value Columbians usually traded at discounts from face value. However, this situation turned about quite radically once the original hoards were dispersed; dollar-value Columbians began to rise in the late 1920s and have apparently not stopped even today. A set of Columbians that cost $16.24 in 1893 would cost about $10,000 today, depending on condition. Not bad for a set that nobody wanted.

The Columbians were sent to the post offices late in 1892 and were scheduled to be valid for postage on January 1, 1893. January 1 was a Sunday, and very few of the stamps were used on that day. Because January 2 was the first day on which open post offices cancelled mail, it has been designated the first day of this stamp. In this very early period, first-day covers generally are accidentals, that is, a postal patron happened to buy a stamp and use it on the first day, and the cover is later discovered by philatelists. First-day covers are known back to the one cent 1851, but before 1910 they usually are rarities selling for thousands of dollars. The two cent Pan American (#295) has been seen by the authors on a May 1, 1901, first-day cover used by Gimbels Department Store to one of its customers with an enclosure of a bill for several hats. Apparently Gimbels sent out hundreds of bills that month in covers that today are worth several thousand dollars each.

The Columbian lower values are much more common used than they are mint. The higher values, above the $1, are about as common mint as they are used, but the mint sell for about three times as much as the used stamps. This is because over the last thirty years, collector fashion has swung to where issues after 1890 are far more popular unused than used. In the 1950s there was not nearly such a difference in price between mint and used.

About 25,000 of the $4 and $5 values were sold, but the overwhelming majority of these are now defective. For some reason, the paper that these stamps were printed on thinned, creased, or got scuffed with the greatest of ease. Ninety-five percent of Columbian stamps have some fault or another. A beautiful-looking set with tiny thins would sell for about one-sixth of what a perfect set would. It is for each collector to decide for himself what quality is worth.

A perfect used block of four of the four-dollar Columbian. In these early days, the differential between the mint and used price of Columbians was not as great as it is today. A collector had this block cancelled for him. He took it to a postal clerk and had the cancellation perfectly applied. And the post office certainly did not mind, for this was $16 for which they would never have to provide service.

The companion block of the five-dollar Columbian.

An imprint and plate number strip of four of the four-dollar Columbian. This sold, with the rest of the set, for $38,000 in 1977. Today, the set would be worth over $100,000.

The Bureau Issues

In 1894, the Post Office Department began having its stamps printed for it by the Bureau of Engraving and Printing (BEP), the same government agency that printed money. The BEP had competed for the 1894 contract, and not only was its price lower, but there was the added convenience of having the work done in Washington near the Post Office Department, allowing greater responsiveness to department needs. The 1894 set contained the same portraits of prominent Americans as the 1890 set, with some values changed and with new values added up to $5. Triangles were added in the upper left corner. Fewer than 6,000 complete sets were sold; of the $5 value, many were used for postage and destroyed. This set is a genuinely undervalued one. As these were the first stamps produced by the Bureau of Engraving and Printing—a good printer but new to stamps—the quality of production, and especially the alignment of the perforations, was poor. Expect to pay great premiums for perfect examples.

In 1895, the Post Office Department ordered the 1894 set to be printed on watermarked paper, which means that philatelists treat the 1895 set as a completely different issue. The paper was watermarked in the sheet with a large repeating double-lined watermark, "U.S.P.S." (United States Postal Service), 16 millimeters

An incredibly rare plate number block of the five dollar #278. Back in 1895 there were but a few plate number block collectors, and of these few, even fewer had $30 to spend for a stamp.

high, in a continuing pattern across the sheet. Stamps frequently have parts of one or more letters watermarking them. These stamps were watermarked because some counterfeits of the 1894 issue had shown up and the postal authorities thought they could better discourage counterfeiting if they printed on watermarked paper. This watermark continued on all stamps until 1910, when a different watermark pattern—using the same letters, but in single line—was used until 1917. Since 1917, no United States stamps have been ordered on watermarked paper.

Part of the reason for the scarcity of the 1894 issues is the quick advent of the 1895 watermarked stamps. The previous issue was in use only a short time and was removed from sale without much warning. Then, as now, collectors usually bought their high-value stamps from the post office at the end of a run rather than the beginning. Why would a collector tie up $5 or more (when $5

A used block of four.

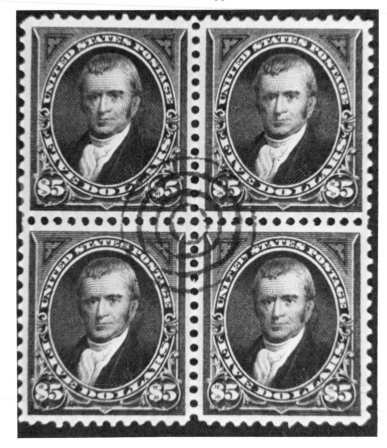

An interesting cover bearing values of the 1895 issue used from the United States Postal Agency in Shanghai, China. America maintained a post office in China until the early part of this century.

bought the average family food for a week, not just a skimpy lunch) for a stamp that would be on sale for years when he could buy it as easily just before it went off sale? Many rarities are created in this way; that is, when the post office quickly and without the usual warning takes an item off sale and collectors who have been waiting to buy it are caught empty-handed. It would seem prudent, then, to buy your high values early in the run. But by the same token, many dollar-value stamps are kept in the post office for five or ten years. To tie up money in quantities of high-value stamps that will show no increase in value until they are taken off sale is not prudent either.

The 1895 watermarked issue (#264–278) is far less scarce than the 1894 unwatermarked, with over 25,000 of the $5 value (#278) distributed.

The 1898 Transmississippi issue (#285–293) is today one of the most popular issues with collectors. The $1 "Cattle in the Storm" (#292) has been voted by serious American philatelists as the most beautiful stamp this nation has ever produced. But to contemporary collectors, still stinging from the unnecessarily high values of the 1893 Columbus set, the issuance of this set seemed positively Machiavellian. The Transmississippi issue contains values up to $2, and though it is listed as having 56,000 complete sets printed, an unknown quantity, but probably 30,000, were unsold and destroyed. For some odd reason, certain values of this set (especially the 4 cent, 10 cent, and $1) were produced well centered and can be purchased in excellent condition without mortgaging the house. But other values (specifically the 8 cent and $2) nearly always are off center. They were all produced at the same time and place, so this is one example of many in philately of experience making a mockery of logic.

The complete set of 1898 Transmississippis (the ten cent is a plate number pair).

THE TWENTIETH CENTURY

The twentieth century is the era of stamps primarily printed for collectors. Whereas in the nineteenth century the views of philatelists seldom mattered at all, beginning about 1890, with increasing frequency, the United States Post Office Department gauged its calculations of stamp issues by how many stamps it believed philatelists would buy.

The quality of stamp production improved radically after 1900 as a result of technological advances in printing and perforating machines, not to mention constant admonishments by collectors. Most twentieth-century stamps can be expected to be reasonably well centered.

The first issue of the new century was the 1901 Pan American Exposition issue. Originally, the Post Office Department planned the Pan American set to contain the same nine values as the Transmississippi set issued just three years before. However, the protests of collectors motivated the department to moderate its plans and issue just six low values with a total face value of 30 cents. The Post Office was being realistic. A new high-value issue, it was feared, would severely reduce the number of collectors.

The complete set of Pan Americans.

The Pan Americans (#294–299) were issued to commemorate the Pan American Exposition in Buffalo. The set was the first bicolor postage stamps issued since 1869, some thirty-two years before, and like the 1869s they are inverts that were produced accidentally. The one-cent, two-cent, and four-cent stamps are known inverted. The set shows transportation scenes with a steamboat on the one cent, a steam train on the two cent, an electric car on the four cent (remember this was 1901), the five cent with a bridge at Niagara Falls, the eight cent showing canals, and the ten cent a steamship. These issues have always been extremely popular with stamp collectors, and were produced by the Post Office Department in surprisingly excellent quality. Thousands of visitors to the Pan American Exposition bought the set as a souvenir and stamp dealers occasionally still get offered the complete set in the little manila envelope they came in when purchased in 1901. If the current owner was lucky, and he stored the stamps in a cool dry place, they are probably still perfect. But a manila envelope is a poor place for a stamp; with humidity and heat, the stamps can easily stain enough to be worthless. Nearly 5 million sets were issued, and many still exist mint. Because of popularity,

The one-cent invert.

The one-cent invert used. Someone bought an inverted sheet and used all of the stamps on envelopes, never realizing that he let what would be today hundreds of thousands of dollars slip through his hands.

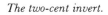

The two-cent invert.

The four-cent invert. The four-cent invert was produced intentionally, so most are known as hand-stamped "specimens."

not intrinsic rarity, a nice mint set could easily set a buyer back $750 or so, and a used set about $100. As with most early twentieth-century stamps, it is harder to find a good example of this set used than it is mint.

In the opinion of many serious philatelists, the 1902 regular issue (#300–313) is one of the most underpriced sets of stamps the United States has ever issued. The set is beautifully engraved, and was the main regular issue set of the post office for seven years, from 1902 to 1909. But the public did not like the stamps (they seldom do). The designs were considered far too crammed with unnecessary detail and the two-cent stamp in particular was criticized severely.

In 1907, a proposal was made for the overprinting of this large stamp issue with the name of the post office at which it would be sold. The proposal was an attempt to reduce the threat of post office theft, which had reached its peak in a robbery of $100,000 worth of postage stamps from a Chicago post office several years before. None of the culprits was ever apprehended, because, it was surmised, the stamps were easily disposed of throughout the country. Overprinting would solve this problem, as the stolen stamps could not readily be sold outside the city from which they were pilfered. Collectors were outraged. A full set of the 1907 issue with

The 1902–03 set.

the same 6,000 overprints that were proposed would have cost a collector over $55,000—a sum that in 1907 not only would have bought a person a house but would have carpeted it, furnished it, fed and clothed its inhabitants, and, further, allowed, with the leftover change, for a stamp collection to be made that included every United States issue to that time! The idea was eventually scrapped, because complex bookkeeping and stamp-ordering procedures precluded its working effectively. A good thing, too. It might have killed stamp collecting.

The 1902–03 issue is quite difficult to find well centered. The values above the 8 cent, with the exception of the 13 cent, all sell for a quantity of money, despite the fact that 260 million of the most common high value, the 10 cent, were sold. Of the thirteen-cent stamp (#308) only 31 million were sold, and of the fifteen-cent, 41 million. Yet the ten cent catalogues mint in the 1981 Scott catalogue at $70, the fifteen cent at $165, and the thirteen cent (of

A plate number block of the one dollar.

The $2 and $5 values were reprinted in 1917 as perforation 10 stamps. They have different Scott numbers from the 1902 perf 12, and are far cheaper.

which far fewer were issued) at only $37.50. This underscores quite accurately the danger faced by collectors or investors when they indiscriminately rely on quantities issued to determine rarity. Because the thirteen-cent stamp was not a stamp that was commonly used, philatelic speculators, (they existed then too) bought up large quantities in the belief that after this issue was moribund, the stamp would prove scarce. And it would have if they hadn't bought them! They tucked away thousands of mint copies; even today this one stamp can be found in quantities. Numbers issued are important, but most significant are the numbers surviving in philatelic hands.

The high values of this set were in use until 1917 and were primarily employed on large, heavy parcels to Russia (that country being in the midst of a civil war, Russian immigrants were sending home blankets and food). Ironically, fewer of the two-dollar stamp (#312) were issued than the five-dollar (#313), but the

The one-cent imperforate.

The five-cent imperforate.

five-dollar sells for about three times as much because fewer survive. These two values were later issued perforated 10, rather than 12, as in this issue, and as such they sell for far less (#479–480).

Three values of the 1902 set (#314, #314A, and #315) were regularly issued to the public in imperforate form. These were intended for use in private coil machines. These stamp machines—which still exist today in drugstores and bowling alleys—could not use the regular stamps because the perforation gauge, measuring 12, is too fine and the stamps tend to split and jam in the machines. Imperforates and imperforate coils were issued to these vending machine coil companies, and these companies in turn perforated them so that they were compatible with their machines. But the imperforate material was made available to the public, too. The 1-cent and 5-cent values are known imperforate, whereas the 4-cent was issued imperforate, but all known copies were privately perforated by the Schermack Vending Machine Company. When buying imperforate stamps, where there are perforated varieties as well, it is always best to buy pairs to prove the imperforate status.

The Pan American series of 1901 had been so popular with collectors and noncollectors alike that in 1904, in a somewhat belated continued tribute to the Louisiana Purchase Exposition held in St. Louis, the Post Office Department decided to issue a series of five commemorative stamps (#323–327). The post office neglected to look at the reasons why the Pan Americans were popular, and as they did not duplicate any of the successful details in the 1904 series, the Louisiana set was a failure. Specifically, the Pan Americans were so successful because they were printed in two colors and because their designs illustrated fascinating vehicles that an increasingly mobile America enjoyed. The Louisiana Purchase issue was only printed in one color and commemorated a historical event that was of little importance to most Americans. The Pan Americans were saved by thousands of noncollectors; the Louisiana Purchase issue so laid in post offices that a postal directive finally had to order postal clerks to fill stamp orders with the Louisiana stamps unless the patron specifically objected.

The stamps themselves, to modern tastes, are quite appealing. Over 4 million sets were printed and sold, and again the numbers game can be quite misleading if applied dogmatically. Of the three cent and ten cent, virtually the same numbers were sold, yet the

The complete set of Louisianas.

ten cent sells for three times as much. Actually, the three-cent is a genuinely undervalued stamp. The ten cent sells for so much more than the three cent not so much because of its scarcity but because many collectors and investors tend to gravitate toward the highest face value stamp in a set.

The year 1907 brought the Jamestown issue (#328–330), which commemorated the 300th anniversary of the settlement in 1607 by Captain John Smith of the Jamestown Plantation in Virginia. The issue has three values, the high value picturing Smith's Indian lover, Pocahontas, the third woman ever to be commemorated on a United States postage stamp. (Queen Isabella of Spain was the first woman, on the $4 value of the 1893 Columbian set; Martha Washington appeared on the eight cent of the 1902 issues.) Originally, Pocahontas was not to be issued, but protests arose from historical groups that the Jamestown set would not be complete without her story.

The complete Jamestown set.

This entire set is very difficult to find in well-centered Very Fine condition, whether mint or used. Seven million of the high value were printed, though you would not know it from the numbers surviving in collectors' hands. Perfect mint sets can sell for as much as $1,000, while off-centered, slightly damaged sets sell for as little as $50. Quality always produces meaningful variations in price, but on no set more so than this one.

After 1907, most United States stamps pictured Washington and Franklin which, in a multitude of variations, remained the chief stamp design until 1922. Collectors often specialize in just this issue. Literature is generally very good for this period, starting with the standard Scott catalogue and Max Johl's excellent book (see Bibliography).

After 1922, the stamps of the United States are almost uniformly not rare, though they are interesting and the Scott catalogue treats them quite well.

United States Airmails

Some of the most popular United States stamps are the Airmail issues. These stamps were issued to pay the increased fee on letters sent by airmail. The first airmail flight (by airplane rather than balloon) took place in September 1911, and was a private flight carrying little mail and covering but a few miles. In 1918, a new set of stamps were issued for airmail service. The six-cent stamp is in an orange shade that often reacts, in spots or in whole, with sulfur in the air to have a deep red brown toning. Unlike coins, toned stamps are considered quite unappealing. Fortunately, soaking the sulfurized examples in hydrogen peroxide can quickly restore the original color by unfixing the sulfur in the stamp. This solution does not work so well for mint stamps, though. Gum is soluble in hydrogen peroxide. Often, it is possible to paint the sulfurized portions of the stamps with the peroxide from a small brush. This is a time-consuming process, but it usually works wonders.

The six-cent orange, like all of the first two Airmail issues, is a difficult stamp to find in well-centered condition, and substantial premiums are paid for perfectly centered, never hinged copies. The stamp is not rare; over 3 million copies were sold.

The sixteen-cent stamp was printed in green. Like the six-cent

The six-cent Airmail stamp.

The sixteen-cent Airmail stamp.

stamp, 3 million copies were printed. As a general rule, more attention is paid to condition on scarce stamps than it is on rare ones. All of the Airmails sell for large discounts from catalogue value if in damaged or slightly damaged condition. Generally, however, the rarer a stamp is, the smaller the difference between perfect and imperfect price. This is because a truly rare stamp is snatched up by collectors whenever it is offered. A much larger supply of the early issue Airmails exists than there is demand. So collectors have a greater degree of choice in the copies they wish to buy, and many gravitate through choice (or because they are advised to do so) toward higher-quality stamps. Perfect, mint, large margin, never hinged Airmails have sold for as much as $1,000, whereas off-center mint stamps with a thin can sell for as little as $75.

The twenty-four-cent Airmail stamp.

The twenty-four-cent stamp is printed in two colors, the blue center bearing a picture of the airplane Curtiss Jenney, surrounded by a bright carmine frame. The stamp is of particularly pleasing appearance, and is probably one of the most famous American stamps for the simple reason that through an unfortunate error, one sheet came out with the center inverted. A plane flying upside down is a spectacular error, and an example of this stamp with the center inverted can sell for as much as $130,000. (The history of the discovery of this error is related in Chapter 8.)

All of the 1918 Airmail stamps were issued in sheets of 100 with 19 straight edges on two sides (one stamp being a double straight edge). But from the number of stamps currently offered with straight edges, rather than this condition being quite common, you would think straight edges were a rarity. This is because so many of the straight-edged copies have been reperforated over the years. Many are identified as such when sold, but a lot of other times they are not. Simply insisting on large margins is not enough. Many of the straight-edged sides were large enough to permit reperfing, with plenty of room left over. (The basic skills in determining a reperforated stamp are described on page 68.) Other than saying that a collector or investor would be wise to buy from an expert, wisdom would suggest that he or she should insist on guarantees and avoid bargains. For years a man who was known to be a reperfer and regummer (since he only bought straight edged and no gum stamps from dealers, and only advertised to sell perfect ones) advertised his perfect wares at 30 percent below the

The complete set of the 1923 Airmail.

prices for which nearly every well-established reputable merchant was selling the same stamps. A bargain can be a bad one! If a dealer's prices are cheap, he may well be on the level; but prudence would suggest checking him out. By the same token, don't be convinced that high prices mean high business ethics.

The 1923 Airmail issue is just as scarce as the first issue. It has three stamps, an eight cent, sixteen cent, and twenty-four cent, and was in use for approximately three years. With all the attention that has been paid to mint stamps the last several years, collectors have been ignoring the real scarcity of attractive used Airmail stamps. Recently, used Airmails have begun moving in price, but they are still far underpriced. First of all, used early Airmails are about as scarce as unused, for the use of airmail service was limited, and many stamps were bought to be kept mint as souvenirs. Secondly, due to the rough handling of the envelopes aboard the early planes, many of the envelopes have bent corners, which creased the stamp. Set prices for perfect examples can run quite high.

The Map set of 1926 was issued to pay the new rate structure put into effect when Congress decided to contract out the airmail service. Before this, government-operated planes flew the mail; but Congress decided to promote the fledgling domestic airline business by contracting with commercial carriers to take the mail, thus giving them assured business on which they could borrow money for expansion. Rates were lowered and this new set was issued. Over 15 million sets were sold. Keep in mind that Airmails are extremely popular. The main reason for this is that less than 100 different Airmail stamps were issued, as opposed to about 2,000 regularly issued ones, and with a few exceptions even a collector of moderate means can get most of them. This set, like most of the Airmails, has shot up in price in the last few years.

Those who did not live through it have no way of comprehending the excitement and exhilaration generated when Charles Lindbergh crossed the Atlantic. The Post Office Department responded by issuing a stamp that was its first issue to honor a living person. It has always been government policy never to picture a living person on a stamp; no doubt this grew as a reaction to early European stamp makers, who put their monarch's portrait on every postage stamp. Americans were quite antimonarchist. Within a few decades of the first American stamp, it became the policy of the

United States government not to commemorate living persons, though some living people have been placed on commemoratives accidentally as part of a picture of something else. The man driving the car on the four-cent Pan American is an example of this; he has little importance to the design, but he was alive when the stamp was issued.

The complete set of the 1926 Airmail.

Lindbergh was being commemorated on this stamp, but the Post Office Department could not bring itself to picture the pilot, so his plane *The Spirit of St. Louis* was shown. Although over 20 million stamps were issued, because of the stamp's popularity with the general population, the number in philatelic hands is far smaller than that.

The most fascinating United States Airmail stamps were not issued for airplane use at all. Since 1928, a number of zeppelin companies had operated transoceanic crossings between the United States and the rest of the world. The three stamps issued on April 19,1930, are among the most popular stamps ever issued. They are far from rare. Over 61,000 sets were issued, but because of the high face value of the set ($4.55) and the timing of the issue coinciding with the beginning of the Great Depression, a large number of sets were unsold. The amount estimated to be in collectors' hands is about 20,000 sets—still quite a few when you consider that their selling price is in the $4,000 to $7,500 range. But from its first issue, this set was popular; the price began rising quickly after it was taken off sale, and it has moved upward steadily over the last fifty years. For the budget-minded, a fifty-cent version of the stamp was issued in 1933 for another zeppelin flight, and trades for about $400.

Below and right: The Graf Zeppelins in plate number blocks of six. This set would sell for about $40,000.

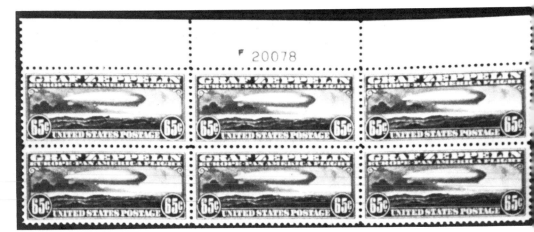

The ten-cent Lindbergh.

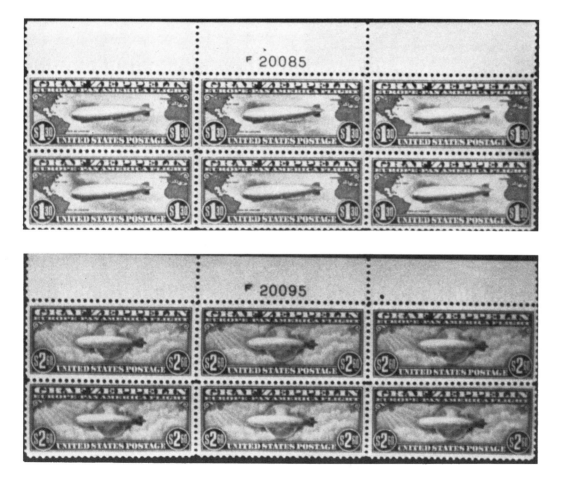

There are more Airmails and there are Special Delivery stamps and Revenues, and local issues, and a whole world of United States stamps that space does not allow us to discuss here. In fact, the Regular Commemorative and Airmail issues just described take up only 25 percent of *Scott's United States Stamp Catalogue Specialized,* so there is much, much more. And every stamp has its story, and its collectors. This discussion has attempted to portray some of the more interesting United States stamps. But remember, every stamp is as worthy of being collected as any other; to say otherwise is not philately.

The fifty-cent Airmail Zeppelin stamp.

6. *The Stamps of Great Britain*

Great Britain was the innovator in postal and philatelic matters. It produced the first postage stamps (see Chapter 2), but the color of the one-penny stamp, the Penny Black, was soon considered unsuitable. The black made it difficult to cancel effectively and the post office in Britain, like its counterparts throughout the world, feared that its stamps were being cleaned and reused.

In late 1840, the decision was made by Rowland Hill and other post office officials to change the colors of the British stamps. A light red brown shade was chosen for the one-penny stamp, and after experimenting with different colors for the two-penny blue, it was resolved to continue printing in blue. A line was added to the design above the value tablet "TWO PENCE," so that this printing could be distinguished from the previous one. The one-penny red stamp was the first-class-rate stamp for Great Britain for thirteen years. About 2 billion were printed and sold, a quantity that has assured their being quite common even today. But the Penny

The Penny Black and Two Penny Blue. The world's first stamps.

Red, as it is called, is a popular stamp, and many collectors own numerous copies as they attempt to plate the stamp, or to collect it by position using the corner check letters. A collector attempting a positioning needs 240 different Penny Reds. The Two Penny Blue 1841 is far scarcer than the Penny Red, indicating the scarcity of double-rate letters, but even of this stamp, 90 million were printed. Two major types of cancellations are known on the 1841 issue: Maltese Cross cancellations and, beginning in 1844, a cancellation called the "1844" type cancel. The "1844" cancels are far more common and are oval-shaped, with numerals inside them. The numerals correspond to an assigned numbering system representing the post office where they were cancelled.

In August of 1841 the first realistic suggestion for the separation of postage stamps, besides the individual use of scissors, was proposed. A correspondent wrote to Rowland Hill suggesting that a deep line might be cut between the stamps when they were engraved, so that in the process of printing, the paper would be pressed into the cuts and each stamp could then easily be parted from the others. But Hill was too preoccupied in advancing his postage stamp innovation and defending his scheme from ruffled bureaucrats to pay the idea much heed. And Hill never thought much of perforations anyway.

In 1847, Henry Archer took up the plea for separations on the sheet, and demonstrated his new invention—a separating machine—to the post office officials later in that year. His early

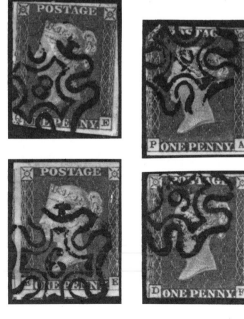

The One Penny 1841. Here are four examples with Maltese Cross cancellations bearing numerals. The numerals in Maltese Crosses refer to the subdistrict post office that cancelled them. They are highly collectable and quite scarce.

A One Penny 1841 with the "1844" type cancel, a numeral between lines, found quite commonly in this issue.

The Two Penny 1841; note the white line added above "TWO PENCE." The cancel, as with all "1844" type numerals in a diamond, is from an Irish town, part of Great Britain before the Irish Revolution.

method was to use rouletting (see page 34). Archer's idea was an innovative one, though it soon became apparent to him that rouletting was not practical for large-scale stamp issuing. The cutting knives wore quickly, and they so cut the bed beneath the stamp sheet that replacements became inordinately costly. In late 1848, Archer abandoned the rouletting idea altogether and developed a perforating machine that produces perforations which both appear and function exactly as on our stamps today. Several trial perforations were made in the ensuing years and some were released to the public. Finally, in 1853, the government paid Archer £4,000 for his machine and his patent rights, a sum Rowland Hill considered wildly extravagant. However, if one were to pro-rate the cost of the patent over the number of times Archer's machine has been used since, the post office purchase must surely rate as one of the great bargains of all times.

While the post office was experimenting with these perforations, some other stamps had been issued, caused primarily by increased public usage of the mails and Britain's growing commerce overseas. Three stamps, all embossed Queen's heads against colored backgrounds, include a one shilling issued in September of 1847 (#5), a ten pence (#6) issued in November 1848, and a six pence (#7) issued in March 1854. These stamps are among the most difficult in all of philately to get in perfect condition. In some places on the sheet, the designs actually overlapped, so that finding examples with any margins at all is well-nigh impossible. And they are often found cut to their octagonal shape, a condition much denigrated by philatelists. Unused examples are rarities.

The first two, #5 and #6, were issued on a paper that had double silk thread running through it, so that each stamp was printed on paper having the double thread line. This was done as an anticounterfeiting measure, the theory being that duplicating the silk thread would discourage would-be counterfeiters and make it easier to apprehend those who did try it. But the silk thread serves a valuable purpose for modern philatelists. The embossed issue was also used on envelopes that were issued by the government, called *postal stationery,* which, in this case, are not nearly as scarce as the stamps. Philatelic swindlers would be tempted to clip the embossed stamp off the envelope and sell it as a postage stamp, were it not for the fact that the lack of silk threads would make this deception obvious. The six pence (#7) does not have a silk thread but was issued on paper watermarked continuously with the letters "V.R."—Victoria Regina.

The first perforated issue of stamps in the world came out in 1854. Each improved perforating machine based on Henry Archer's design was able to perforate 400,000 stamps per day. They were run by steam, and at first five machines were employed, giving the printing office the capacity to perforate 2 million stamps per day. The early experiments with perforations and small die types account for the next fourteen Great Britain catalogue-listed stamps issued over the ensuing four years. It should be noted that until recently the British Post Office's stamp-issuing policy was probably the most conservative in the world. Indeed, the One Penny 1841 remained in use until a perforated version appeared. Some die variations in the mid- and late 1850s make for collectable varieties, but the 1864 One Penny stamp was

The Embossed issues. Note how closely together the stamps were printed. These stamps are great rarities when they are fine quality like these examples.

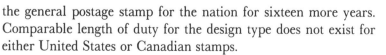

the general postage stamp for the nation for sixteen more years. Comparable length of duty for the design type does not exist for either United States or Canadian stamps.

The first perforated stamps were perf gauge 16, and it was soon discovered that perf 16 gauge perforation separated far too well. The closeness of the holes meant that postal clerks had to be extremely careful lest the stamps should tear apart in their draw-ers. Even with care, the stamps were difficult to work with and to transport in quantity. A little later a gauge perf 14 was tried, which spread out the holes a bit; apparently both perf 14 and perf 16 were used coincidentally. Many perforation varieties exist of these early perforated stamps, including double rows of perfora-tions, partly perforated stamps, and even completely imperforated stamps. Furthermore, the centering of the perforations on the stamps—or, as philatelists usually misrefer to it, the centering of stamp within the perforations—was wretched. It is almost impos-sible to find one of these early perforated stamps in which the per-foration holes do not touch the design of the stamps. Still, the innovation was well received. The public cared little about how its stamps were centered. And there were not enough collectors yet to make the complaints that render the quality control job at the post office so unpleasant.

Finally, in 1855, Perkins, Bacon & Petch, the printers of Great Britain's postage stamps, wrote to the Inland Revenue, which administered stamp printing, and said it was time that a new die was made for the One Penny stamp. The new die would have more deeply cut lines, which would show the Queen's head off to finer contrast. As an added bonus, the deeply cut die would last longer, and so require that less plates be made. Apparently, the government was also ready for a change. In less than a week it responded that Perkins, Bacon & Petch should begin preparing the new die, which was issued shortly thereafter.

FOUR CHECK LETTERS

The British Post Office had evidence that some postal users were clipping uncancelled parts of stamps and reassembling them on letters to pay postage. Finally, in 1857, the post office got around to ordering stamps with four check letters, the letters in an order reversed from the top to the bottom. The check letters make it much more difficult to use uncancelled portions of stamps convincingly.

The One Penny 1864 with four corner check letters is one of the most popular specialty stamps in the world. Many collectors who do not even collect general issues of Great Britain maintain a holding of this stamp. It is about the easiest stamp in the world

The One Penny 1864. The plate number of the stamps is in the scrollwork in two places, behind the Queen's head and across from her nose. The block of four was printed from plate number 122.

to plate, for not only do the check letters tell a collector the position of the stamp, but in the tablets at the right and the left of Queen Victoria's head are engraved the plate number of the plate that the stamp came from. One hundred fifty plates of this stamp were used over its long life, and with the exception of the last plate, plate 225 (which was only in use for four weeks), none of them is particularly scarce, except for plate 77. Plate 77 was rejected as defective, but a few examples have surfaced. Edward Bacon, one of the printers, believed that these very rare plate 77s were trial printings from the plate, made before it was destroyed. A few of these trials somehow managed to get out to post offices and be sold to postal patrons. Examples of plate 77 are among the major rarities of worldwide philately. Many hearts have stopped beating when a collector confused a plate 177—a very common plate—in which the "1" was obliterated by the cancellation, with a plate 77.

With some 150 plates and 240 stamps in each plate, a collector would need 36,000 different examples of the same stamp in order to complete a plating and positioning of this stamp (though only 240 are needed for a positioning alone). Until recently, in quan-

The surface-printed issues of 1855–75. A selection with both small corner check letters and the later large corner check letters.

tities the stamp sold for less than 1 penny a piece. Now they probably sell for about 15 cents. There were over 30 billion printed during the life of the stamp. Although statistics of this kind are difficult to correlate, this is probably the largest printing of a nineteenth-century postage stamp, and may well be the largest printing of any stamp ever.

The very quality of the line engraving by Perkins, Bacon & Petch, which proved to be such an effective anticounterfeiting device, also greatly concerned the Post Office Department. It was felt that the line-engraved stamps could withstand a veritable bath of ink eradicators and the design would still be as clear as ever. The department was very concerned over this potential (mostly imagined) cleaning and reuse. It therefore instructed another printing company, the De La Rue Company, to begin printing a four-pence stamp typographed, that is surface-printed, with a somewhat fugitive ink. Anyone attempting to take a cancellation off one of these surface-printed stamps would soon find himself with the design leaving the stamp before the cancellation did. The first surface-printed British stamp was issued in 1855; it continued in use, with some watermark changes, until 1862, when a new issue was called for.

The 1862 issue was also a surface-printed one and incorporated a 3-pence, 6-pence, 9-pence, and 1-shilling value, as well as a revised 4-pence of the previous issue. The reason for the revision on the surface-printed stamps was the same as it was on the engraved, that is, to place corner check letters in the four corners so as to prevent a patron from clipping two uncancelled halves from used stamps and pasting them together on an envelope, thus defrauding the government out of revenue. The surface-printed issue with small corner letters are extremely attractive and well-designed stamps. Their colors were well chosen and they have retained much of their freshness even until our day. The nine pence is an especially scarce and undervalued stamp. It was used to pay the postage on prepaid letters to India, Australia, and South America. Undamaged covers bearing well-centered stamps are very scarce, and because of the remote destinations and lack of stamp collectors in the non-European continents, few of the nine pence were saved. It is an excellent stamp. Like all nineteenth-century Great Britains, the nine pence is exceptionally difficult to find well centered; and well-centered, mint, original gum examples are a combination that is seldom seen.

In 1865, the same set was reprinted on the same watermarked paper (small emblems in each of the four corners of the stamp), but this time around the corner check letters were greatly enlarged because it was felt that the tiny letters on the previous issue did not especially discourage cutting and reuse. Again a 3-pence, 4-pence, 6-pence, and 1-shilling value were issued. However, a great rarity, a ten pence on emblem-watermarked paper, was also inadvertently issued, when the next set, the 1867 set, was printed, and is actually an error. It is a later stamp accidentally printed on an old batch of paper.

The 1867 set was basically the same group of stamps printed on a paper with a new watermark—a pattern that looks like a rose. A number of values were issued over the next thirteen years and these are among the most interesting stamps of the British Commonwealth.

For decades, throughout the nineteenth and well into the early twentieth centuries, the British operated post offices in all corners of the world. These were different from the post offices that their colonial governments ran, which issued their own stamps and pro-

The British Post Offices Abroad. This stamp was used in the British Post Office at Malta. Philatelists can tell that by looking at the cancellation number, A25.

The high-value Victorias.

vided internal postal service for the countries involved. Rather, the British Post Offices Abroad, as they were called, were far-flung extensions of the British Postal System. They used Great Britain stamps, and operated as a British Post Office in such places as Chile, Peru, and Thailand. British postal officials cancelled British stamps used there with distinctive cancellations, usually bearing a letter followed by two digits. Thus, A26 is Gibraltar and C51 is St. Thomas. The internal post offices mostly used three-digit cancels with no letter. In all, there were hundreds of British Post Offices Abroad cancellations. Often letters are seen bearing both the postage of the country where the British Post Office Abroad was, so as to pay carriage to the British Post Office, and the British postage, to pay the British carriage. Used Abroads are a fascinating specialty, and indeed the use of British stamps abroad was so widespread that most stamps thus used sell for only a modest premium over a regular usage. Covers are a different story and can command substantial premiums.

In 1867, Britain began issuing a series of high values that would give it by 1882 the highest face value stamps in the world. In that year a five-shilling stamp was issued which had a face value of £5 (at that time approximately $1.30). The United States had issued several ninety-cent stamps, so this British high value was not unprecedented. Indeed, one Liverpool firm complained that it frequently sent postal packets requiring postage of 70 shillings and more. With a one-shilling stamp being the highest stamp provided, the firm complained that the package was so full of stamps there was no room for the address. The five shilling came out in 1867; a ten-shilling and one-pound stamp both in 1878. In 1882, a five-shilling, ten-shilling, and one-pound stamp, all with a different watermark, came out, as did one of the highest value stamps ever issued, a five-pound stamp with an astonishing $26 face value. In 1882, that was a great sum of money. The Five Pound stamp remained in use until 1903, and during its life about a quarter of a million were printed and sold. An odd fact of life about very high value stamps is that a much larger proportion of them are saved than of the used lower-value stamps. They were a curiosity rarely seen by people when they were used, and so were tucked away by even noncollectors.

The stamps of Great Britain are a complex field, assembled by collectors in Great Britain to a degree of specialization that this chapter can only begin to suggest. In particular, English collectors

The 1883 set, missing the lower values. The values above the 2 pence in this set were printed in a light shade of green, making bright, colorful examples desirable and rare.

The complete set of the 1887–92 issue. Most of the values are bicolored. This is an attractive set that often can be found in nice condition.

The high-value Edwards.

love to classify minor varieties of shade. Indeed, rarely do Americans or Canadians seek out anything but the most striking of shade varieties, whereas the British find eminently collectable the minor variations of shade that occur even between different printings of the same stamps.

British stamps are a wonderful specialty, worthy of an inquisitive, inquiring collector at any stage.

The 1913–19 issues, called Sea Horses by philatelists because of the allegorical design. These are popular stamps among collectors.

The 1929 Universal Postal Union Commemorative Issue. An extremely popular stamp that sold for under $100 in 1970, shot up to $2,000 in 1979, and recently has found its level at about the $1,200 range.

7. *The Stamps of Canada*

The stamps of Canada are among the most popularly collected stamps anywhere in the world. Their designs have been chosen with near-uniform excellence, and their execution as a printed product is first rate. Canadian stamps up until World War II were all engraved, and have been designed and printed by the best bank-note-printing firms in the world.

The first Canadian postage stamps were issued in 1851. They were printed by the New York printing firm of Rawdon, Wright, Hatch & Edson, who were also at the time printing the United States postage stamps. Rawdon, Wright, Hatch & Edson were about the most advanced printers of their time, and had been used before by the Canadian government to print debentures. Three stamps were contracted for: a three-penny stamp, picturing a Canadian beaver; a six-penny stamp, showing Prince Albert, the Royal Consort; and a twelve-penny stamp, showing Queen Victoria in black. There was criticism of the designs and the printing

The three-cent Beaver of Canada— Canada's first stamp.

The twelve-penny Canada on a cover—Canada's greatest rarity. This example would have sold in 1980 at about $100,000.

of the first stamps; the twelve-penny stamps were especially disliked, and their high face value was rarely called for. Accordingly, today this is one of the world's great rarities. Only 51,000 were printed and delivered to the Canadian postal authorities; and of these, only 1,510 were sent to post offices. Even less were sold.

The 1851 issue, as it is listed in the catalogue, was printed on laid paper (see page 28). This is the major difference between the

1851 issue and the 1852 issue, which was printed on wove paper. The laid lines in the paper of this 1851 issue are extremely difficult to see, and even experts must resort occasionally to determining which set is which by shade of color alone. The 1851 issue was generally cancelled with a cancellation of concentric circles around a point, called by philatelists a *target cancel.*

The use of laid paper did not last long. Laid paper often does not take a design well in printing, primarily because of the variance of thickness in the paper. The stamps tend to print very lightly, and this was especially true of the twelve penny. Furthermore, the problems caused by laid paper extend to the adhesive as well. The 1851 Canada issue was roundly criticized for not sticking to letters when moistened. The first three-penny stamps on wove paper (#4) were delivered to the Canadian postal authorities in April 1852. This stamp is considered a highly specialized field of its own by some students of Canadian philately. They identify no less than five distinct paper varieties, including three types of handmade paper and two types of machine-made paper that came into use in 1857. Most Canadian collectors gladly content themselves with one example of the stamp.

Between early 1855 and mid-1857, rate changes forced the issuance of three additional stamps. The ten pence shows Jacques Cartier, and is in a lovely dark blue color; it was for use on letters going by British packet to Europe. The 6½ pence sterling, 7½ pence currency stamp is one of the first, and indeed along with the ten penny mentioned above, one of the only stamps to accommodate monetary difference within the wording of the stamp. The rate it paid could be paid either way, in currency or sterling. This stamp used the same design as the twelve-penny stamp that is so rare. The one-half-penny stamp is in a dreary shade of lilac and was used primarily on newspaper wrappers. Because of this, it is exceptionally scarce in perfect condition. Stamps on newspaper wrappers were often used to reinforce the seal of the wrapper on the paper and thus were ripped in two when the paper was received.

By November 1854, the Canadian Post Office had heard of the great revolution in stamp production that had just occurred in England: a perforating machine had been invented, and stamps now came with little holes in them so that they did not have to be

The ten-pence Cartier of 1855. Note that the postage can be paid two ways: 8 pence sterling (at the top) and 10 cents currency (at the bottom).

The three-cent Beaver perforated. The poor alignment of the perforations was a result of the primitive equipment.

cut from the sheet. The Canadian Post Office authorities wrote to their stamp printer, Rawdon, Wright, Hatch & Edson, about incorporating this advance on future Canadian postage stamps. They received back a tart note saying that such a request was impossible. And indeed it was—the only perforating machines were in London. Technicians on the other side of the Atlantic could only guess at how it worked. By 1858, the Canadian postal authorities were finally informed that a perforating machine could be obtained. Shortly afterwards, at an additional charge of 5 cents per 1,000 stamps, perforated stamps were supplied. The early perforating machines were extremely primitive, consisting of perforation rows running in one direction through which the sheet of stamps had to be run twice, once for the vertical rows and a second time for the horizontal. The space adjustments for the rows, as the Canadian stamps were not square, had to be altered with each run through the machine. Knowing this, it is amazing that we find any well-centered examples of the first perforated issue of 1858 at all. But we don't see many. The perforated pence issues are the half penny, three penny, and six penny.

When postage rates were changed in Canada in 1859, no new design was prepared. The printers merely changed the value from 3 to 5 cents and reissued the stamp. The poor alignment of the perforations allowed part of the American Bank Note Company's imprint (successor to Rawdon, Wright, Hatch & Edson) to show.

THE DECIMAL CURRENCY ISSUE OF 1854

As can be seen on the Canadian stamps pictured, the monetary system of Canada was figured in both currency and sterling. The variations were irksome, and the calculations of who owed what to whom and in what currency were ended in 1859, when the Canadian government enacted laws giving Canada a decimal currency system. The stamps that were printed were a one cent, ten cent, twelve and one-half cent, and seventeen cent. In 1864, a two-

The one cent 1859.

cent stamp was added. Almost none of the Decimal Currency issues are rare. Yet centered, undamaged copies are extremely difficult to find.

The ten cent was given no less than twenty-five printings during its life; its shades varied from black brown to a color that is almost red. It is said of this stamp that no two stamps bear an identical shade, so greatly do they vary in color. The black brown is the rarest shade and is listed as a separate number in the Scott catalogue. Great confusion exists over these shades—prudence would dictate buying the rare black brown shade only from a reputable dealer and with a certificate of genuineness.

The ten cent 1859. Not one stamp in 10,000 is centered this well.

The twelve and one-half cent, a reworked version of the earlier twelve-penny stamp (the great rarity), with the same design though a new color, value, and perforation.

The 1859 perforated reissue of the ten pence 1855. The value was increased to 17 cents.

THE 1868 LARGE QUEENS

The Large Queens, as philatelists call the 1868 issue, was the first stamp issued by the Dominion of Canada created on July 1, 1867, by the British North American Act. Immediately Ontario, Quebec, New Brunswick, and Nova Scotia were united. In 1869, the Dominion purchased the Hudson Bay Company's considerable lands, and when British Columbia joined the Dominion in 1871, Canada was a cross-continent country. A new stamp issue was planned and printed, as befitted this new Canadian nation, by the British North American Company, located in Ottawa.

The first Dominion of Canada issue is called the Large Queens by philatelists because they show a large portrait of Queen Victoria, and to distinguish them from the later Dominion issue of smaller format known as the Small Queens. The 1-cent, 2-cent, and 3-cent values of the Large Queens come on laid paper, but they are great rarities that way. Collectors should check all copies of these stamps to see if they have any of these rarities. Occasionally, they may be found in ordinary collections. All of the Large Queens are known on watermarked paper, though they were not regularly ordered that way. Rather, these watermarks are papermaker watermarks and read either in double letters or in script. Both watermarks were applied across the sheet, so that only portions may appear on each stamp. Most stamps do not show the watermark, but collectors should keep their eyes open for this variety. The half-cent and the fifteen-cent ones are great rarities on watermarked paper.

The Small Queen issue commenced in 1870, though most values of the Large Queens remained in general use and were slowly replaced by Small Queen issues in the ensuing twenty years. The

The Large Queens of 1868–76.

primary reason for the change was that the demand for stamps in Canada proved to be very great. The smaller format allowed the printers to produce more stamps on the same press in the same amount of time, with the same amount of paper and ink. The Small Queens duplicated the values of the Large Queens, with the addition in 1893 of a 6-cent value and a 20-cent and a 50-cent in a slightly different format. The Small Queens are highly specialized in by some philatelists. For the most part they are relatively inexpensive, and are even cheap in used condition. Shade varieties and perforation varieties abound. There are many reentries and double transfers that collectors like to look for. *Double transfers,* as noted earlier, are slight doublings of certain portions of the design caused when the plate is originally made and the die is imperfectly rocked in. *Reentries* look exactly like double transfers. Again, they are a doubling of a portion of the design, this time caused when the plate is reentered so as to strengthen the design on a worn plate. For those with a good pair of eyes, each reentry and double transfer can be identified according to lists of characteristics discovered by philatelists of the past.

A target cancel, often found in the early stamps of Canada.

The 1870–93 Small Queens, designed to reduce costs and expedite printing as more stamps could be produced per sheet of paper.

Two exceptionally centered examples of the Small Queens.

A used ten-cent Small Queen with part of the printer's imprint showing at left.

In 1897, the Canadian Post Office signed a stamp printing contract with the American Bank Note Company, though the stipulation was that the printing had to be done in Canada. The 1897 Jubilee issue had as its justification the sixtieth anniversary of the reign of Queen Victoria. Some have suggested, however, that it was patterned after the 1893 Columbus Exposition issue which had proved so lucrative to the United States Post Office. The values, with the Canadian addition of a one-half-cent stamp, are virtually the same, and the similarity in style is no doubt due to the printing being done by the American Bank Note Company. Virtually the same number of high-value Canadian Jubilees were ordered as were ordered of the dollar-value Columbians. But they didn't sell as well, and of the three-dollar and four-dollar stamps, less than 10,000 were reported sold. The low values of the set soon sold out to postal users, though deliveries of high values continued to be made until 1901.

The higher values of the 1897 Jubilee issue.

The 1897 issue of Canada is called the Maple Leaf issue. Victoria was on this stamp again, as she was to be alive for four more years. She reigned all told for sixty-four years, and had the distinction of having been on more postage stamps from more countries than anyone at that time. In recent times, it seems likely that Queen Elizabeth II has or shortly will surpass Victoria in this postage stamp derby and become the person who has had her face on more stamps than any other. (Elizabeth's reign has not been nearly as long as Queen Victoria's, but countries issue so many more stamps now than they did then.) The Maple Leaf issue contained eight values and was extremely well printed. (At this time, the United States had just taken the printing contract away from the American Bank Note Company, and the Bureau of Engraving and Printing was having much difficulty producing well-centered stamps whereas the American Bank Note Company had really

The 1897 issue is more popularly known as the Maple Leaf issue.

mastered the stamp production process.) Almost all the 1897 Maple Leafs are at least reasonably well centered, the colors are bright and fresh, wisely chosen and deep in tone, and the gum has retained a high degree of freshness.

In 1899, a group of three-cent stamps were surcharged "two cents" when the first-class postage rates changed a penny downwards at the end of 1898. These overprinted stamps are not scarce. In 1898, the set was modified slightly, and numerals, indicating the value of the stamp, were placed in the bottom corners so as to make the values of the stamps easier to read for busy postal clerks and the French-speaking patrons of the Canadian post. The set was expanded to include a 20-cent value.

In recent years, as topical or thematic collecting has become increasingly popular, so has one of Canada's most interesting stamps. It is the issue known as the Imperial Penny Postage, put out after the Imperial Postal Conference of 1898 when a number of members of the British Commonwealth took the bold step of lowering their postage rates to 1 penny (British), which was 2

Canadian cents. The rate was to take effect on Christmas Day
1898, and a new stamp was prepared to commemorate the change.
The stamp marked the day of the change, "Xmas 1898," and
showed a map of the British Empire. The black part of the stamp
is engraved, and the colors, lavender and carmine, and blue and
carmine on the two different varieties, are printed by topography
(a process similar to lithography). As a Christmas topical, it is the
first ever. As a history of postage topic, it is an important issue.
And it is one of Canada's most beautiful stamps. The price, especially for attractive examples, is surprisingly reasonable.

Queen Victoria died on January 29, 1901. When its next stamp
was issued in 1903, Canada replaced Victoria's picture with King
Edward VII's. The design characteristics of the Edward stamps
are similar to the earlier Victoria ones, except that the maple
leaves in the top corners have been replaced by Tudor crowns.
The maple leaves are still shown, but moved down behind the
numerals of value. The high values of this set are extremely desirable in well-centered, mint condition; in recent years, collectors
have begun to seek used examples of the twenty cent and fifty cent,
as the prices of the mint stamps have risen too fast.

The 1898 set.

The 1898 Imperial Penny Postal issue—one of Canada's most interesting stamps.

As a side point but a salient one, the prices of used stamps and mint stamps never rise in tandem. Rather, when the price of a mint stamp rises more quickly than the collector market can support, collectors begin to turn to used stamps. The mint stamps then become dormant for a time in terms of price rise, as without a large body of collectors around to support the rise, the market cannot continue its quantum leaps. Then used stamps begin to move upward for a while, and percentage-wise, they catch up with the mint stamps. This happens until the used stamps no longer continue to be perceived as a bargain relative to mint stamps, at which time the market for mint again becomes active. This is not a rational, thought-out strategy on the part of collectors; rather, it is the result of thousands of collectors each attempting to get the most for their money.

The year 1908 was the 300th anniversary of the founding of Quebec, the first permanent settlement in Canada. The post office issued a set of eight stamps called by collectors the Quebec Tercentenary. The set is beautifully engraved and has long been a favorite with collectors.

After 1908, the stamps of Canada are quite straightforward and are treated excellently by the general stamp catalogues. Canadian stamps have been among the most popular in the world during the decade of the seventies and into the eighties. This is due to a number of factors, not the least of which is their nearly uniform high standard of production. Add to that the great appeal of all British North American stamps in Great Britain as former members of the British Commonwealth; and, further, there is a strong native Canadian market.

The 1903 Edward VII issue. The fifty-cent stamp has a Montreal precancel.

But the biggest reason for Canada's rise in popularity has been its discovery by American stamp collectors. This was caused primarily because of the Canadian stamps' relevance and assessibility to American collectors, and the fact that, with few exceptions, the bulk of Canadian stamps sell at reasonable prices for their rarity. A person of average means can assemble a collection of Canada that is 98 percent complete. Indeed, there are only a few Canadian stamps that sell for over $1,000 in mint condition, and only a few that sell for over $100 in used condition. Canadian stamps, then, are getting more and more popular among Americans priced out of their home stamps. Canadians collect their own stamps, too, manifesting the general nationalistic choice of most collectors.

The 1908 Quebec issue.

The 1912 King George issue.

8. *Rarities*

~~~~~~

Rarities attract the most attention in the stamp world. They are really no more interesting than common stamps, but they receive more press. Dollar values are something that everyone can understand. Philatelic speakers who go before nonphilatelic groups to talk about philately and stamp investing usually find themselves ignored until dollar amounts are put on the items. Then the speaker finds an active interest: "$10,000 for *that,* wow!"

Probably the foremost popular rarities of philately are the 1918 United States Airmail Invert, the 1852 British Guiana One Cent Magenta, the two-cent Hawaiian Missionaries, and the Mauritius "Post Office."

THE AIRMAIL INVERT

Few people get the kind of shock William Robey did one day in 1918 when he walked up to the stamp counter at the Washing-

A block of the Airmail invert.

ton Post Office and asked for the best centered sheet of the new twenty-four-cent Airmail stamp that they had. Robey was a stamp collector, though as a twenty-six-year-old stockbroker's clerk he had little money for his hobby. But he had made arrangements with friends to send them covers franked with the new stamp, along with some mint copies from the sheet he was going to buy. They never got them.

The sheet that the postal clerk handed to Robey had the center inverted. Robey saw it right away; the clerk did not. United States law is very clear on this matter. Anything that you buy from the post office is yours to keep, but if the postal clerk discovers the error before you have paid for the item, he is required to take it off sale and return it to the postal inspectors. Robey's hands shook as he paid for the sheet. After removing it from the counter, he asked the clerk if he had any more items like this one, with the airplane upside down. The clerk asked him for the sheet back, now discovering the error. When Robey refused, the clerk called his superior. Soon post offices from New York to Washington were closed while clerks shuffled through stacks of stamps attempting to find additional error sheets so that they could be destroyed before being issued to the public.

The 1918 Airmail invert was not the first inverted-center stamp that the government ever unintentionally produced. Three values of the 1869 issue and three values of the 1901 Pan American Exposition issue are known inverted, and most of the previous inverts are scarcer, in some cases far scarcer, than the 1918 Airmail invert. But there is something spectacular about this invert. It has an immediate appeal. And remember, most people in 1918 did not trust airplanes anyway.

Robey immediately announced his discovery, and was inundated with offers to buy the sheet. He wasn't shy about soliciting them, either. He took a trip from Washington to New York, stopping at stamp dealers along the way, and receiving offers for the sheet. Robey finally sold the sheet for $15,000, a fabulous sum in that day for an error of a stamp still in production. The buyer was Eugene Klein, the famous Philadelphia stamp dealer.

When a stamp is in production, as the 1918 Airmail invert was, there is no way of determining how many of the errors might turn up. As Klein laid out his $15,000 for the sheet of 100, or $150 per stamp, at a time when only a few of the world's greatest rarities sold for more, he was betting that no more sheets of the error would be found. Klein had more faith in the Bureau of Engraving and Printing quality control than we have today. And Robey? After he got his $15,000 for the sheet for which he paid $24, he became a philatelic celebrity of sorts, speaking at stamp clubs, telling his story over and over again.

No one really knows what Klein had in mind in buying the sheet. He promptly took out an advertisement in a stamp magazine offering the error for sale as singles, indicating a desire to break up the sheet. The price was $250 for a single and $175 for a straight-edged single. But the price at which they were offered would have netted him only a small margin of return considering the amount of work involved in making 100 sales. Perhaps Klein wanted the publicity. Or perhaps he wanted to attract the one buyer of stamps who had the resources and inclination to purchase the sheet. Colonel Ned Green was the son of Hetty Green, the famous financier. (Hetty Green was a noted miser: when Ned Green was young, he had a leg infection and Hetty refused to take him to a competent specialist as she did not wish to spend the money. Green lost his leg!) Green was an avid collector of everything from yachts to women. One of his more inexpensive hobbies was stamps. He heard of the sheet, and after the advertisement offering the stamp for sale as singles had appeared, but before the sheet had been broken up, a private sale was arranged. Green bought the sheet for $20,000.

Klein was a reliable, decent sort of man, perhaps the best dealer of his day. He convinced Green to break the sheet, and to slowly offer some of the stamps for sale, a move not naturally in Green's hoarding disposition. Klein's reasoning was twofold: he wanted collectors to have the opportunity to own this rarity; and secondly, without any activity in buying and selling of the stamp, Klein told Green that he risked losing out on his investment as the error would soon fall from public view and hence desirability. This second argument impressed Green (who was after all Hetty Green's son) and the sheet was broken up into a variety of blocks and singles. Green numbered each stamp lightly in pencil on the back, corresponding to its position, moving across the top row from left to right, then continuing in the same way down the sheet. Only about 85 of the 100 stamps can now be accounted for. No doubt some of the remaining items are owned by philatelists who view anonymity as the best protection against theft. A block of four was stolen in 1955 while it was on display. But some of the stamps—and we don't know how many—have been lost. Some say they sunk on one of Green's yachts; and others report that Green's collecting room resembled a barn, where perhaps a few were simply thrown away by some over-diligent maid.

Errors are made by the Bureau of Engraving and Printing every year. The most common of these are perforation errors, either adding an extra row of perfs where they shouldn't be (not an important error), or omitting a row where there should be one (an important error). Coil stamps, that is, stamps issued in rolls, are the stamps that are most often found with missing perforations. This is because their being wound in rolls makes it difficult for the quality inspectors to see whether they have been perforated. Imperforate coils sell for between $15 and $250 a pair, depending on the scarcity of the item. A collector must have a pair to prove that the coil is imperforate. This is insisted upon because a single stamp could just be clipped down to resemble an imperf. Color errors and inverts are far more scarce, but even modern color errors that are scarcer than the Airmail invert have trouble selling for more than about $1,000 per stamp. The Airmail invert has a history of desirability that these other items do not.

Stamp dealers are constantly besieged with calls from collectors and noncollectors alike who have bought something funny from the post office. Most of the items are minor perforation or color shifts. A *perforation shift* is a stamp where the perforations are not where they should be. A *color shift* is a misregistration of the colors so that the design appears fuzzy. Unless a shift creates a bizarre effect, such items do not find favor with philatelists. But suppose you find a real error, a missing color, or even an invert. Prudent stamp dealers advise clients who do discover such things to exercise extreme patience and care in disposing of them. The reason for this is that there are few Eugene Kleins around any more. Until dealers know how many of a given error will surface, they will be reluctant to pay a great deal for it. In modern times, some errors have come out in huge quantities. Most buyers assume an error will be common until the cumulative data of a few years proves otherwise.

When speaking about errors, collectors must keep in mind the difference between errors of execution, which are rare, and errors of design, which are not. Sometimes a designer improperly researches his subject and a person is shown in a setting that is historically incorrect. Such historical anacronisms abound on stamps, as do wrong names for places and pictures. But unless the stamp-issuing authority ceases production once the issue is discovered, and corrects it, the error of design in and of itself does not cause the stamp to be rare.

The Airmail invert is an error of execution, not of design. Its price, as America's most popular stamp, has been meteoric. By 1939, a copy had realized $4,100. During the war years, the stamp market was relatively quiescent as the country had more on its mind than hobbies, no matter how fascinating. By 1969, the stamp was selling in the $30,000 range. Five years later saw it in the high $40,000s. In 1978, the first copy sold for $100,000, and in 1980, a block of four that had sold four years before at $170,000 was traded for half a million dollars. Prices of Airmail inverts, like all stamps, are dependent on the quality of the specimen. Defective or straight-edged copies bring about half the price of perfect ones.

Paying the price of a nice house for a tiny piece of paper strikes many people as odd. In 1918, when Green bought the entire sheet of 100 for $20,000, the *New York Times* stated editorially what most noncollectors have thought more than once: "At this time there are several better uses for $20,000 than the purchase of a set of stamps which, except for a printer's error, would be worth just $24 in the open market." Still, there is something exciting about owning something of which fewer than sixty can be bought (there are the "lost" inverts, and about twenty-five in institutions). And the Airmail invert, expensive as it is, cannot even lay claim to being the most expensive stamp in the world. That honor belongs to our next specimen.

THE BRITISH GUIANA ONE CENT MAGENTA

In April of 1980 the unique One Cent Magenta sold at auction for $935,000 ($850,000 plus 10 percent buyer's commission). The first price that it traded for between philatelists was 6 shillings or about 50 cents. And the man who bought the stamp for that price only did so because the seller was a young boy and he wished to further the youngster's interest in philately. Neither of the two, the discoverer or the first buyer, knew its rarity or its story.

British Guiana, a small country that is now part of Guyana on the northeast coast of South America, had since 1853 ordered its stamps from the Waterlow printing firm in London. In early 1856, the colony apparently ran out of stamps. This simple occurrence is all that we know with certainty, and we know it because the one-cent and the four-cent stamps that Waterlow supplied are not found cancelled from February until October 1856, no doubt the period during which the regular issue was out of stock and on reorder. Beyond this, all information on the world's rarest stamp has been pieced together from what seems likely.

When the post office ran out of stamps, it turned to the only printer of any status in the colony, the firm of Baum & Dallas who printed the *Official Gazette,* the newspaper of Demerara (now Georgetown), capital of British Guiana. Even by printing standards of the 1850s, Baum & Dallas were backwater printers. They had no engraving capacity and had a hand press. Stamps were ordered with newspaper type letters. The picture of the sailing ship on the stamp is a stock cut that Baum & Dallas pilfered from the "Shipping News" page of their newspaper. The stamps

The British Guiana One Cent Magenta. The ink marks on the face are the initials of the postmaster of Demerara who signed these stamps as they were sold.

present a level of crudity in their execution that is almost unrivaled in philately. The one cent and four cent are textbook examples of ugly stamps, poorly designed and executed. But they are rare. The one cent to date is unique and the four cent has but a few specimens.

The one cent was found by a child named Vaughn, who in later years remembered it as being on a small letter from which he had soaked it off. This is the only part of the British Guiana rarity saga that is probably wrong. The one cent paid the newspaper rate, so the likelihood is that Vaughn found it on a wrapper of some kind, not an envelope. The use of the one cent on newspapers or newspaper wrappers accounts for its rarity—even if as many one-cent stamps were sold as were four-cent stamps, wrappers were rarely saved and stamps so used in the pre-1870 period are generally quite scarce. Vaughn did not even find the stamp until 1872, sixteen years after it was issued. He was unimpressed with the specimen; it was clipped diagonally and faded.

The man to whom Vaughn sold the stamp was the most prominent collector of British Guiana, a Mr. N. R. McKinnon. McKinnon kept the stamp for about five years, gradually becoming aware of its scarcity until his research led him to believe that it might well be unique. He sold his collection, including the One Cent Magenta, to an English dealer for £120. The dealer, Thomas Ridpath of Liverpool, sold the British Guiana One Cent Magenta to the one collector with the means and desire for the stamp—Baron Philipp La Renotière Von Ferrary—for a sum believed to be in the neighborhood of £150.

The British Guiana One Cent Magenta's fame rests on its distinction of having realized the greatest sum at the Ferrary sales held after World War I. Ferrary's collection was an achievement; virtually every rarity of any stature was included, often in blocks and on cover as well. There were hundreds of volumes. Numerous other stamps elicited interest during the Ferrary sales, but the most attention was paid to the British Guiana. Including a bidder's tax, the stamp realized over $30,000, which when you compare it to the $3,000 realized for the Sweden 3-skilling banco error of color (also unique), shows the awe in which this stamp was held.

At this time, there were several major collectors in the world with the means and the interest to purchase this stamp. But foremost among them were Arthur Hind and Maurice Burrus. Hind was a New York State industrialist; Burrus controlled tobacco in Belgium. When the lot opened up on the floor, the bidding was quite hesitant. Then the war began between Burrus and Hind's agent: $8,000—$10,000—$15,000—$30,000; and there it stopped. The auctioneer looked once at both the buyers, and twice, sold! Both bidders claimed victory as the room hushed. It was unclear, even to the auctioneer, who had given the last bid. He was about to reopen the lot, which might well have gone to even dizzier heights, had not Burrus then bowed out and allowed Hind's agent to buy the stamp.

In 1951, nearly thirty years after Burrus had attempted to claim the stamp for $30,000, the famous collector publicly made a charge that the British Guiana One Cent Magenta was in reality a fake, made up of a four-cent magenta which had had the "FOUR" and the "S" at the end of "CENTS" chemically removed and a "ONE" inserted. Mr. Burrus had made these charges privately prior to the 1937 resale of the stamp when it was submitted for *expertization* to the Royal Philatelic Society. The stamp was examined in every way possible. The opinion of the greatest collegium of experts was that work of the sort that Burrus suggested could not have been done on this stamp, and that the stamp was and is unquestionably genuine. It seems odd that Burrus would have bid on a stamp that he believed to be a forgery, or that the feisty Belgian would have waited fifteen years after he lost the stamp to first make his claim. To these charges he replied that he bid on the stamp because before the auction he had overheard Hind's agent talking about what a high bid he had on the stamp and, as a tease, he decided to run it up. Then, he said, out of deference to its owner, he decided to make no claim about the stamp's stature until Mr. Hind was dead.

After Hind's death, the British Guiana remained unsold for a period of time. In about 1939 the stamp was sold to Frederick Small, for a sum rumored to be around $50,000. Small was not known to be the owner of the stamp until he sold it in 1970. The British Guiana One Cent Magenta was then purchased for $240,000 by a group of Pennsylvania investors who, like Small, had little interest in philately. They sold it in 1980 for $935,000 ($850,000 plus a 10 percent buyer's premium) and currently the new owner is unknown.

THE MAURITIUS "POST OFFICE"

In 1847, Mauritius was the fifth country in the world to issue stamps. The British had taken over the island only thirty-seven years before, in 1810, largely as a result of the fact that the French had used the island as a base to interrupt British shipments to and from India during wartime. The population of the colony was French, Creole, and Indian; English, though spoken by government officials, was not the language of the people.

The government order that called for stamps fixed the postage rates at 2 pence for internal letters and 1 penny for intra-city letters. The stamps were crudely engraved, as the only person in the colony with any experience in engraving was a partially blind watchmaker who had never been a professional engraver. Five hundred of each value were ordered and, after some delay, delivered. In the left-hand panel, the engraver put the words "POST OFFICE" rather than "POST PAID" as the stamps were ordered. When the stamps were reordered, the wording was changed to "POST PAID," and it accounts for their extreme rarity. However,

A rare cover bearing both the one- and two-penny Mauritius "Post Office" stamps. Note that inscription in the left portion of the stamps.

the "POST OFFICE" stamps were needed quickly, because the Governor's wife, Lady Gomm, was holding a fancy-dress ball at Government House and the stamps were wanted to send out the invitations.

Those that Lady Gomm did not use were placed on public sale, and due to the popularity of the innovation, the stamps sold out very quickly. Most were used locally, a few on letters to France, and at least one to India. Of the approximately thirty specimens of the Post Office Mauritius, slightly more than half are the One Penny Red, and the remainder are the Two Penny Blue. Oddly, the stamps were not discovered until 1864, by a French collector who traded them away because her albums did not have a space for them. In 1865 the items ended up, as did so many items at the middle of the last century, in the stock of the Belgian dealer Moens. Moens bought the original One Penny and Two Penny for about $35—a fabulous sum in 1865 for postage stamps—and sold them a few months later for about $100, as the world gasped at what lengths stamp collectors would go to satisfy their mania. Today, the stamps would sell together for $500,000.

In stamp collecting there are a number of rarities that sell for comparatively small sums. In certain specialized areas of philately, the collectors do not bid up to high levels on even the greatest rarities. Some town cancellations on early United States stamps and some perforation varieties are virtually unique, yet they sell for extremely modest sums. A rare item is an expensive item only if it is desired by a wide group of collectors and only if it has a history of high prices. Rarity alone does not make high price.

Indeed, even within the narrow confines of the high-priced rarities themselves (the megabuck wonders, as they may well be called), there is great inequity in price. The Airmail invert, for which there are eighty-five or so known examples extant, sells for about the same as one of the two Mauritius stamps, of each of which only about fifteen are known. And indeed, the very rare Z grills of the United States—major stamps from a major collecting country—sell for about the same as the Airmail invert, despite the fact that they are each at least about twenty times as rare.

Obviously, supply and demand affect prices, but that says so much that it says nearly nothing. Those contemplating the purchase of a high-price rarity would be wise to research the price trends and history of the specific stamp. For philately has its fashions, too, and what one generation desires another may well eschew.

THE HAWAIIAN MISSIONARIES

Christian missionaries probably had more success in Hawaii than anywhere else in the world. The first missionaries came to the islands in 1820, and by 1825, the Hawaiian king recognized the ten commandments as the basis of his legal system. Soon the Hawaiian language was formulated as a written discipline by the missionaries, and, as further testimony to their zeal, in 1835 the islands outlawed public drunkenness.

The islanders were essentially an agricultural people, whose polytheistic religion was filled with idols and taboos. The early Hawaiian concept of an afterlife was peculiarly unpleasant: most Hawaiians believed that evil spirits slowly ate them after death. The missionaries, besides offering education and law, gave the Hawaiians a religion that would at least provide a pleasant after-life for people who had been good. The new religion was embraced, and within thirty years, only vestiges of the previous religion remained.

An exceedingly rare cover bearing the two-cent and five-cent Hawaiian Missionaries along with two U.S. stamps.

An agrarian society has little need for government mail service, and a society that has not learned to write has even less. This was the situation in Hawaii before the missionaries came. But the missionaries did require a post, both to communicate with each other from island to island and to communicate with family, friends, and coworkers back home. The first stamps were produced under a postal reform act of 1851 and were issued in October of that year. Three stamps were produced: a two cent, five cent, and thirteen cent. The two-cent and five-cent stamps, when used to the United States, had to have additional United States stamps applied to them or else they would arrive postage due. The thirteen-cent stamp would pay the postage through, though money would later be exchanged between the United States and Hawaiian postal services, and the stamp would be cancelled "US Hawaiian Postage Paid." All three of these stamps are called the Hawaiian Missionaries because they are found almost exclusively on missionary correspondence.

The three stamps were printed on an extremely thin, hard paper called *pelure* by philatelists; pelure paper resembles an onion skin as much as it does paper, and it is extremely brittle. Although the missionary stamps were issued in 1851, they were unknown to the community of philatelists until 1864. Even then, many philatelists considered their status to be questionable, until information on their issuance was ferreted out of Hawaii some years later. The jury was out on the two-cent Hawaii, by far the rarest of the three, until the mid-1890s.

One of philately's most fascinating stories relates to the two-cent missionary. (And it does not stem from the fertile brain of Agatha Christie, either!) In June of 1892, a French collector, Mr. Gaston Leroux, was discovered murdered. There was no sign of a break-in at his Paris apartment, and though the drawers of his desk appeared to be rifled through, there was no evidence that any of Leroux's considerable possessions had been taken. The apartment was searched and researched for clues until finally the motive for the crime was discovered—Leroux's two-cent Hawaiian was missing from his collection.

Even in 1892, a two-cent Hawaiian was worth about $2,000. Police fanned out through the city, checking dealers' shops and notable collectors to see if anyone had been offered the stamp. Suspicion (the reasons are not clear) fell on another prominent collector, one Hector Giroux. A detective of the police force pretended he was a collector, joined the Paris Society, learned about stamps, and eventually befriended Giroux. After some months, the detective feigned an especial interest in the rare Hawaiian Missionaries, particularly the precious two cent. Soon the pride of the collector Giroux overcame his prudence and he showed the policeman the two-cent Missionary. He was arrested and eventually confessed to the crime. Giroux had the money to buy the stamp, he said, but Leroux would not sell.

Philatelists have long wondered whether Giroux should have been made to stand trial. Among a jury of collectors, "temporary philatelic insanity" would have been a reasonable defense for the crime. As stamps from a United States possession, the Hawaiian Missionaries have great popularity, and of the fourteen specimens that are known of the two cent, only about half now exist outside philatelic museums and so can be bought by a collector. In November of 1980, two examples of the two cent were sold from the collection of Royohei Ishakawa, who in recent years has created perhaps the finest United States and United States–related stamp collections. Both copies realized over $200,000 when they were sold, which represents an increase of 100 times the 1900 price.

9. Stamps—The Investment

~~~~~~

Financial theory, much like political or military theory, evolves over time. The past is usually quite clear, but the future is exceedingly difficult to hypothesize about, let alone predict. All of us are so involved in the current investment strategies that few are able to step away for long enough to see how the economy is changing.

For example, in England for decades before 1850, among the best investments were forms of interest-bearing bonds. In a non-inflationary economy, 5 percent per annum interest was not a bad return. And the English tax rate of that period was so low that the 5 percent netted the investor only a little less than that. For the individual investor, probably the greatest opportunity for a large-yielding investment return since the advent of insurance trading companies to ensure trade with the East was the invention of the steam engine. Huge economies could result because coal and wood would now do the work of men and horses. But the machines had to be built and fuel had to be dug, and this presented tremendous opportunities for capital. Perhaps the greatest fortunes ever made were done so in both England and America financing and producing the Industrial Revolution of 1800–75.

At any moment in time, there are wonderful opportunities on the stock market. But, on the whole, over the last twenty years the shares of most companies have been comatose, and there is little certainty that future movement will be upward. The high-technology stocks have been in vogue, but they are short-term strategies and are good only until some higher technology stock comes along. The oil stocks have grown tremendously in the last ten years, more as a result of inventory profit and higher volume due to higher prices than because of any intrinsic managerial excellence. And with few exceptions, the oil companies have had difficulty channeling these profits into constructive investments outside of the energy field. Indeed, the energy companies are even having trouble investing in other areas of the energy production field, so that profits will remain strong long after petroleum ceases to provide the overwhelming percentage of our total energy. The oil companies seem to act like the landed gentry of old, sitting pretty on top of their estate, built years ago, raking up profits that they have had little to do with earning.

Even if you are a smart investor, the tax rate in the United States and in most of the world, when combined with the inflation rate, makes it extremely difficult for a person with capital to stay even, let alone get ahead. This is why companies have shifted income disbursement patterns from dividends to income retention (and expansion) so as to produce greater net worth. The higher net worth of the company hopefully results in a higher share value, which allows investors to take their profits at capital gains rates when the stock is sold, rather than as prejudicially taxed dividends. This is unfortunate, as companies that are expert in some area of business and technology are often quite inept at others, and only expand into other areas because of the pressures produced by the tax code.

Gold is an extremely popular investment today, and because of uncertainty in the world, will probably continue to be so. But it must be remembered that in the 100 years between 1860 and 1960 gold proved itself to be a very poor investment, the price only a little more than doubling in a century—an uncompounded rate of 1 percent per year, which could easily have been quadrupled at

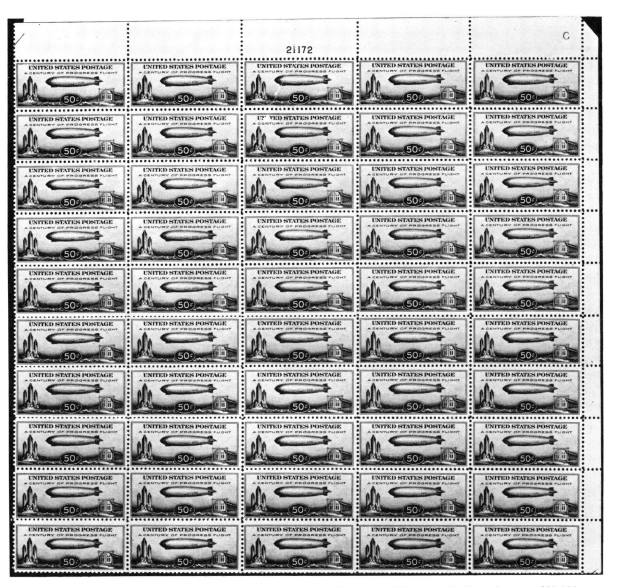

A sheet of the 1933 Airmail. Anyone could have bought this then for $25, or in 1970 for $1,500. Today's price—$20,000.

any bank. Gold buyers continue to hope that hard money will someday be the choice of world government; but short of monetary collapse, it's hard to imagine any government voluntarily advancing this position. After all, money is a commodity, and government is its producer. The ability to print money gives governments great power, which they will probably always retain.

STAMPS AS AN INVESTMENT

For the last eighty years, the investment potential of fine collectable stamps has not been lost on the worldwide philatelic community. Numerous references to the elementals of supply and demand and their effect on the burgeoning stamp market are found in English journals of the 1890s, and in American journals not much later. For the last decade, stamps have been an excellent investment medium, with rare United States stamp prices increasing at an average compounded rate of 15 percent. In 1979 the rate

The Germany Posthorn set as a new issue in 1951 sold for about $15. Today, it catalogues for over $2,500.

The 1929 Canada Blue Nose *quintupled in price in the decade of the 1970s.*

was 40 percent. It is difficult to go back and evaluate prices of eighty years ago to see how stamps fared at the turn of the century. For one thing, grading standards were much less strict, and auction catalogues frequently did not grade stamps at all. Thus, we have a record of widely varying prices for the same items. However, just using the Scott catalogue price (which represents the average price of what would be considered a fine specimen of a particular stamp), a broad selection of the most commonly traded scarce United States stamps shows an increase of about 100 between 1900 and 1981. Foreign stamps, at least those from major collected countries, have done as well, and in some cases substantially better.

The Disadvantages and Advantages of Stamp Investing

There are both advantages and disadvantages to stamp investing. Many of the disadvantages are not readily apparent, so they will be discussed first.

Stamps are perishable: After all, they are made of paper. And unlike stock certificates, which are also engravings on paper, stamps do not represent or give title to the item of value. They are in fact, like art, the item of value themselves. Stamps can be affected by light, heat, and humidity, and must be stored in a proper place. Though one can, and should, insure stamps against destruction and theft, it is extremely difficult to insure them for wear and tear. Many investors place a stamp in their safe-deposit box immediately after it is purchased so that the handling danger may be mitigated. With proper skill and practice, though, anyone who can tie shoes can learn to handle stamps properly, with little danger of man-made faults. But remember, nibbing a perforation even slightly will adversely affect value.

Stamps are not "leverageable": Many investors, especially those who dream of making great killings, prefer to increase the investment clout their money gives them. This is often done by leverage, which cannot be used for stamps. But most stocks can be margined up to 50 percent of their value—a form of leverage that means if you buy 100 shares of General Motors at $100 per share, you need only put up $5,000, not $10,000, which is the cost of the stock. The brokerage firm will lend you the rest, usually near or below prime, and keep the stock for security. Suppose the value of the stock goes up 20 percent in a year (excluding interest deductions and dividend payments, which alter the subject a bit), you have made $2,000. But when you figure the $2,000 was made on an investment of $5,000, which is all that you had to put out, your effective yield is 40 percent. Think of "leverage" as a shorthand way of referring to the use of borrowed money where the object purchased is the collateral. But, of course, leverage, like a pendulum, can drift both ways; you may find a relatively small drop in a highly leveraged investment, such as the commodities market, wiping out your entire investment in a very short time.

Anybody who has ever bought a house and paid for it with a mortgage has used leverage. In fact, if it were not for the high degree of leverage available to homeowners (that is, the low down payment of only 20 percent of the total amount of purchase), home ownership would not be nearly the fine investment it is thought to be today. When prices rise, there is nothing so financially rewarding as working with someone else's money. But, of course, screws do turn.

And the inability to leverage stamps as an investment means that the pure investor, who would buy potato spud futures in Chad if they were the best investment, has not entered the stamp market. For stamps must produce yields greatly in excess of leveraged investments in order to be competitive with them. So as long as the strict investor stays removed from the stamp market, collector pressure will push up stamp prices, but with nothing like the velocity that we would see if the potato spud bugs got into the game.

Stamps could be a disorderly market: Because stamps have no intrinsic value other than their face value, which is usually quite negligible, there is a risk in an economic downturn of having a commodity for which there is no buyer. This is mentioned as it is a fear of investors, although it has never actually happened. During the Great Depression of 1929–39, stamps lost a percentage of their value, but never reached the depths of common stocks. At their nadir, most stamps sold for about 65 percent of the pre-Depression price, compared with the Dow Jones average reaching about 10 percent of its pre-Depression price. So while it may seem that stamps might be unmarketable in a depression, the one historical test indicated that virtually everything was unmarketable in the Depression, and stamps were better than nearly all conventional investment items.

Stamp investing is not for everyone: It is not for older people who need dividend income to supplement social security and pension income. Stamps are not a good short-term investment, either. The spread between what you buy an item for and what the same dealer will pay you for that item is high, usually at least 20 percent, and often quite a bit more. But have you ever checked stockbrokers' fees for small share trades of a few hundred dollars? And that is the level at which most stamps are traded. Stamps are still an old-fashioned hobby business, and though this is slowly changing, dealers still work on the old, low-volume, high-markup principle so prevalent in the hobby world. True, too, is the fact that each stamp must be graded individually and this is a time-consuming process.

Right now a plan is germinating in a number of people's minds for a closed-end mutual fund that would invest in stamps. Basically, the fund would be capitalized by issuing shares, which would then be publicly traded, based on the value of the stamps that are owned. An amount of trading would be done by the fund, of course, so as to liquidate items that have already made their upward move, and replace them with stamps that are so poised. The fund could function as its own sales operator, buying and selling directly, and so could lower its purchasing and liquidation expenses. This idea has seen discussion over the last couple of years, and might soon become a reality.

People who have made large profits in stamps share several distinctive traits. By and large, they are people who have maintained modest collections throughout their lifetime and who, at about the age of forty or fifty, because of rising income and declining real expenses, begin to have more money (and time) to put into their hobby. They usually buy stamps primarily as a hobbyist, but they are generally optimistic about stamps as an investment. They plan to hold their stamps for at least ten years.

There are several advantages to rare stamp investing:

Rare stamps are truly rare: On an average day, 250,000 shares of Boeing are traded on the New York Stock Exchange, which represents about $10 million changing hands on a single day's trade of a single stock. Ten million dollars placed in the stock or bond market means very little, but in the rare stamp market, $10 million is a huge amount of money. To buy nearly every United States stamp issued to 1890 (not one of each, but every one!) would cost but a few hundred million dollars (at 1980 prices), just 10 percent of the dollar amounts purchased on the New York Stock Exchange on a single day. Of course, as the buyer of the stamps came closer and closer to this goal, price rises would push the attainment beyond his reach. But even so, rare stamps are incredibly rare. Items of which only a few thousand exist often sell for a few hundred dollars and seldom for more than a few thousand. The stamp market, despite phenomenal rises over the last decade, is looked at by some investment people as a fantastic new field where prices have only just begun to rise.

A work of art: Philately is one of the few investments where the buyer can reap aesthetic as well as financial rewards. Many people have turned to rare stamp investing for strictly pragmatic, financially remunerative reasons, and have ended up becoming hardened philatelists for whom the investment potential of stamps became secondary. The irrational love of stamps is one of philately's greatest investment strengths. For it means that when short-term market fluctuations push down the price of a certain stamp, or when a stamp reaches a price plateau at which it appears it will remain for a few years, there is no rush of sellers to further depress prices because the holders of these stamps are keeping them for more than pure investment reasons.

Some investors love philately's tiny size: The large pension funds, mutual funds, and trust funds are in virtual control of the stock and bond markets today. Philately remains one of the few areas in which an investor with as little as $50 per month to spend can assemble, over the course of years, a significant holding of great value.

How to Invest

All the desire in the world will not get you very far in stamp investing without the knowledge to go with it. And unfortunately, as with every field, there is no easy way to obtain knowledge. But there are a few shortcuts.

Beware of price shopping. Price shopping is an excellent way of saving money when you are searching out a brand-name dishwasher, but it can be dangerous when you are buying a stamp. Suppose you see the same stamp graded the same way by two stamp dealers, but one is hypothetically priced at $500 and the other at $300. The novice's brain will begin ringing, "I've got a bargain," whereas the more advanced collector-investor will only hear, "Danger . . ." In the highly competitive stamp business, it is unlikely (not impossible but unlikely) that two stamp dealers will have high-grade philatelic material at such widely varying prices. Variations of 20 percent may exist, but much more is improbable. Be especially careful if one price is much lower than the prevailing price usually charged for that item. No doubt the dealer with the very low price will proudly tell you that his is so low because he recently rooked some widow. But even if the dealer does have the smell of a skunk, is it realistic to assume that he would pass on the results of his dishonesty to you? More likely, it is not only the widow who gets ripped off. People who are sold repaired or altered stamps usually paid no more for the stamps they bought than the stamps were really worth. It's just that the buyers thought they were getting a bargain.

A collector-investor's stamp room should look like a library. He should subscribe to stamp papers and magazines, auction catalogues (with prices realized), and price lists. There is no substitution for knowledge.

Two Investors

Frederick Small was, like many others, a stamp collector during his childhood in Australia. But when he went off to fight in World War I, his parents gave his collection away during some general house cleaning. To Small, it was no matter; the collection was virtually worthless.

As an adult, Small had no interest in postage stamps, but he believed that they possessed investment potential. He remembered the catastrophic inflation of the 1920s, especially in Germany, where currency became almost worthless. Wheelbarrels of money were required for food marketing, and inflation was so rapid that employees had their salaries renegotiated twice a day. The mark went from 3 to the dollar to 3 billion to the dollar in three years. That's inflation!

In 1940, Small turned to a philatelic investment counselor whom he trusted. He began to collect British Guiana not because he liked the stamps of that country, but because the country appeared to him and his adviser to be undervalued at that particular point in history. Collecting, like clothing, has its fashions, and it is rare for any country or stamp to remain permanently out of favor.

The decision to collect British Guiana was also affected by the fact that the country issued the rarest stamp in the world—the unique One Cent Magenta. Small bought the stamp in 1939 for around $50,000. He sold it in 1970 for $280,000 at public auction. Even after commission, he realized a profit of over 500 percent, exceptional in the low inflation period of 1940–70. The syndicate of Pennsylvania investors who resold the stamp in 1980 for $935,000 gained over a half million dollars in ten years, more than enough to cover the inflationary decade of the 1970s. But Frederick Small was never a collector. "I didn't consider my stamp col-

The Amelia Earhart overprint of Mexico. This is a popular stamp with only 430 printed. It sells for about $2,500 each, depending on condition. Hypothetically, an investment firm could buy all of them for about $1 million, far less than the amount of IBM stock traded in a single hour on an average Wall Street day.

lection as a hobby," he said before his death, "but as an investment, just like shares of stock." Neither did the Pennsylvania syndicate consider the collector value of this stamp. They, too, were hard-nosed investors looking for a profit.

Roger Demmy was different. He was not a wealthy man, but he loved stamps. He had been collecting them since 1905: he saved every one he had ever gotten, and he was obstinate enough to collect just the countries he liked. In the 1930s, Demmy bought first issue Japanese stamps. This was the era of "yellow peril" fever, and dealers were happy to sell Demmy all of the classic Japan that they had for 10 cents and 15 cents each. Today, these stamps sell for upward of $300 each. Demmy had hundreds of them.

Demmy worked all of his life as a night watchman at a chemical plant in Chicago. He was a serious philatelist who also collected Sweden and Great Britain. Until 1960, Demmy never spent more than $20 a week on his collection. When he died in 1975, his stamps were worth over $200,000. The reason—simple! He bought stamps for virtually nothing that increased in value thousands of times. Not foresight as much as luck; even if Demmy's stamps went nowhere, he would have loved them anyway. But he bought classics, rare stamps for which there was demand.

Small and Demmy represent different investment positions. One is the pure investor, the other the hobbyist. They both made substantial profits as they each learned what they were doing, sought expert advice, and had long-range plans.

INVESTMENT STRATEGIES

Since 1960, people have become involved with stamps who have little interest in them as philatelists, but rather have an active interest in them as investments. Such people have usually approached stamp investment in one or more of the following ways.

Creating a Collection

Some investors used to look askance at creating a collection. After all, they would tell you again and again, they were not collectors. After a time, however, it began to be apparent that making a collection was not only fun, it had some pretty smart investment strategy associated with it. First of all, simply buying stamps that are touted in the philatelic and financial presses has risks. Only stamps that are available in quantity or have already made a significant wave are ever mentioned in the media. This makes sense—the media are only interested in facts, so far as they can tell them, not hunches. But the best investment ideas for the future are only hunches today. Rare stamps that have not yet made their move are often offered to a collector because there is no investor market for them yet. They can be bought advantageously then. Furthermore, by creating a collection of a country or even the world, an investor is, in essence, spreading his risk. It's nice to have zeppelins when they jump from $3,000 to $6,000 a set. It's not so nice to have them when they hold steady for a period of time or even fall in price. A collection of 1,000 stamps made over

Frederick Small—perhaps the world's first investor.

a period of years has, at any given time, stamps in it that are going up and stamps that are stable. And when liquidation time comes, what is to prevent you from selling only that part of your holdings that you believe will show low growth for the near future and holding that part that you most believe is going to rise further?

Most investors who create a collection as a safe philatelic investment also combine it with a little old-fashioned speculative hoarding as well. Every philatelist has some favorite stamps that he believes are going to go up. Even the most dogmatic adherent to the theory of spreading your risk buys a few of his favorites. Remember there are several hundred quality investment stamps in United States philately alone, and the economic history of these stamps over the last eighty years indicates that some of them are always moving quite substantially. A spread holding might miss some spectacular growth that can be produced if the investor buys absolutely right; but a spread holding, the history indicates, has always risen in value.

Cornering the Market

Another investment strategy is a modification of the old cornering-the-market theme. This is for high rollers only, affords considerable risk, but also can be used to advantage by astute speculators. Essentially, the scheme entails buying all of a specific philatelic item that you can and through this means pushing up the price. For example, you and some partners decide that zeppelins selling at $5,000 a set are too cheap, and you purchase all that you can at that price. Approximately 250 sets come on the market each month, so you can see that this would take some money. But the nice part about this plan is that you don't end up buying all of the sets (indeed, usually only a fraction of them), because at every increased incremental level there are some sets that sell to collectors and other investors at slightly more than you are willing to pay.

There are several problems with cornering the market. First of all, as the price increases, your money purchases fewer and fewer of the items that you are trying to control. At the same time, because of higher price levels, collectors who bought their sets years ago seek to liquidate at the new higher level, thereby increasing (sometimes dramatically) the number of the particular stamps that are offered each month. As a general rule of thumb, if you are considering cornering any philatelic market, assume your capital needs as follows: You'll need to be able to buy about 20 percent of the known supply of the item, at a price that you should assume will average out to be about twice what it was when the item started.

Actually, the cornering-the-market game is much more profitable to the side players than it ever is to the chump who sticks it out from beginning to end. By watching price movements, and determining whether a control group seems to be developing, a sophisticated investor can buy along with them, liquidating with modest profits well before the bubble bursts. Remember, in stamps as in most other investments, those seeking big profits usually receive for their efforts big losses; whereas those who are satisfied with more prudent results often do quite well.

The Study of Stamps

But there is another almost foolproof stamp investment strategy. It is not for everyone, as it requires patience and knowledge: the scheme requires an investor to immerse himself totally in the study of stamps and find a philatelic specialty that really excites him. The clever investor then obtains all the auction catalogues he can, visits stamp shops, and slowly acquires interesting items for his collection, which he mounts and displays. The stamps and covers in a specialized collection often have a symbiotic relationship to one another: two $50 covers next to each other frequently produce a $200 page. The clever investor makes his collection over a period of years, and sometimes so fools the world into believing that he loves his stamps as a hobby that he fools himself as well. Then he does some very uninvestor-like things like turning down huge profits on his collection because he loves it. More and more, investors are discovering that while they came to philately for the profit, they stay for the fun.

MYTHS OF THE STAMP MARKET

When people read the Salamon Brothers report, which maintains that stamps were the third best investment over the decade of the 1970s, ranking behind oil and gold, they expect to see a high percentile increase in the price of stamps on a year-to-year basis. Such an impression is misleading. Most people who avidly watch stocks or commodities know that investment items trade in a relatively narrow band most of the time. Then, for whatever reason—good news in the case of most stocks and bad news in the case of most commodities—they sometimes shoot up 20 to 30 percent in a very few days. And often they jump down the same way. Slow, steady progress in financial matters simply does not occur in the trading, though the long-term results may make it seem that way.

Stamps are much the same. A stamp will trade in a very narrow band, then in a matter of a month or two move up 50 percent or more, to remain relatively quiescent for the next interval. This much we know about the stamp market. What we don't know are the two things we most want to: we do not know when a particular stamp will move, and we do not know how much it will move. But we have a theory. The collector is in reality the stamp market. It is he, for whatever irrational reasons, who buys this otherwise worthless piece of paper and puts it in album never to sell it until dotage or death. One group of market analysts watches the larger stamp dealers, who sell primarily to collectors, to see what they have in short supply—for it is collector demand that has pruned these dealers' supply. Such items usually go up in price. Theories on how much a particular item will go up once it has begun its move abound; unfortunately, they do not predict much better than chance.

Some people live with the mistaken notion that you have to be rich to invest in stamps. Now there are many different evaluations of what constitutes rich. The average family income in the United States in 1980 is almost $20,000. If you are average and you have kids in college or braces (or, God forbid, both), you probably do not have enough money left over after expenses to invest in a movie and popcorn, much less stamps. But as your children gradually go onto someone else's payroll, and your home mortgage in real terms begins to demand less and less of your take-home pay, even a person of modest means can invest in stamps.

If someone can spend even $20 a month on stamps, he can derive a reasonable investment return from them in addition to the pleasures of collecting. From a strict standpoint of investing, a person spending only $20 per month should never buy more than one or two stamps each month. When you purchase lower-priced stamps, you are buying almost all dealer handling. To prove the point, modern United States plate blocks, which most retailers sell at prices ranging from 85 cents to $2, sell wholesale in quantity for just a fraction over the face value of the stamps. To a collector, this does not matter; the later stamps that he buys—which are cheaper and the price of which represents mostly labor—he chalks up to his hobby. The earlier stamps that he has—which are expensive and have significant growth potential—he chalks up as an investment.

Stamps are an exceptionally poor short-term investment. If you go to sell your stamps, you will often get only 70 percent or less of their retail or resale price, which is considerably lower than conventional investment instruments. If you sell your stamps at auction, the commission will end up being 20 percent of the ultimate sales price, so you see that a relatively long holding period is the only way stamp investments will work. When you buy a stamp for $100, it is immediately worth $70 or less; and even with 15 percent per annum growth it will take nearly three years to pull up again. But by compounding, assuming the 15 percent per annum holds, you should be able to sell the same stamp for a 40 percent profit after five years, and 175 percent profit after ten years, all taxed at the preferential capital gains rate.

WHAT NOT TO INVEST IN

There are billions of stamps, and only some of them should be part of a reasonable investment strategy. In general, investors should try to stay away from the new issues of any country, be it United States or foreign. Many people have made huge gains by buying up quantities of modern, newly issued stamps that have later turned out to be scarce. But the risks are too high, and the possibility of postal authorities reissuing the stamps if supplies run short always exists. If an investor had bought every new issue since 1960 from major countries, he would still be unable to sell the entire group at a profit. And that is true even though many stamps have sprung up in value. The bulk of philatelic items, perhaps 95 percent or so, never show any significant financial gains.

Above all, stay away from United States new issues. There is an appeal to some investors in purchasing mint sheets from the United States Post Office, in that the sheets have a certain face or postage value, and so the investors assume there is little downside risk. And this is true. But there is little growth potential, either. Since 1950, out of the over 900 stamps that the United States Post Office has issued, all but perhaps 30 sell for either a few percentage points above or below face value. The reason for this is that mint sheets seem like such a perfect investment to people that thousands buy them, creating a supply that is far in excess of demand. Stamp dealers routinely use the stamps from the 1950s on their mail as they cannot sell them in quantity at even face value. And if dealers cannot sell these mint stamps at face value, you can bet they will pay a lot less than that if you come to sell them.

There has been a great deal of general media publicity and advertising recently over a whole variety of specially prepared, illustrated, even personalized first-day covers. Such covers have a price of between $2 and $4, and are mailed monthly to subscribers as the stamps come out. The first-day cover clubs produce a handsome, artistic, and educationally satisfying product. Unfortunately, the investment potential of these particular first-day covers is small. A collector can service his own cacheted first-day covers, through the United States Postal Service, for about 50 cents; the wholesale value of first-day covers in quantity when bought by a dealer is about 35 cents each. When bought at this price, there is some investment potential. But when purchased on subscription from the national "clubs" that offer them, the covers must increase in price over 700 percent before you can get your cost back! Furthermore, should you decide that the convenience of the clubs is worth the expense, avoid the temptation to "personalize" your first-day covers, that is, to have your name and address placed on them. America's modern penchant for labeling everything from eyeglasses to dungarees does not find favor with philatelists. Addressed first-day covers since 1945 have traded at about 50 percent of unaddressed.

For investment potential, as a general rule, investors should stick to established, responsible countries such as (though not limited to) the United States, Canada, Western Europe, the British Commonwealth, and Japan. These countries have a strong base of native collectors, who have created an intrinsic demand for their indigenous stamps through strong and weak economic times. There are many countries now, in Africa, Asia, and Latin America, that use their postal services in an attempt to earn foreign currency. The stamps routinely commemorate American, English, and European events, even though these countries just as routinely frustrate our goals in the United Nations and on the world scene. The stamps are attractive and for the most part well designed and executed. But they are produced solely for export; there are few collectors in those poverty-stricken nations. So unless worldwide collectors reverse their 140-year trend of preferring the stamps of their own nation, there is little likelihood that the $10 and $20 face value sets of most third and fourth world countries will enjoy booming resale.

Ultimately, the future of stamp investing comes down to the future of stamp collecting. Stamps have no intrinsic value and no commercial applications; their value is all perceived value as a collectable. Several factors do seem to point to a stronger and stronger collector base in the industrialized world. Stamp collectors break down into essentially two age groups, the teens and the over forties. While some people retain an interest in stamps throughout their life, the pressure and constraints of career and family building during their twenties, thirties, and forties makes most collectors' interest passive in these years. They begin to collect again in the later third of their life—and it is this group's demand that has caused the increase in stamp prices. The simple demographic fact of the post–World War II baby boom means a gigantic increase ahead in people with the time and means to resume collecting. This group will make the period from the 1980s into the early part of the next century the golden age of philately, even if increased publicity makes them collect in no greater numbers than did the generation preceding them. We should add to this the fact that women seem to be beginning to create collections of substance and value for the first time. Previously, though many women collected stamps, they were rarely serious collectors or investors in rare stamps. But this situation has begun to change radically.

It is the opinion of most people who counsel stamp investors that philately is not the best investment. It has problems of leverage, storage, and high spreads between bid and ask that many alternate investment forms do not have. But stamps do not have to be the best investment, for they are not, in the final analysis, primarily an investment. To most people who collect and invest, they are primarily a hobby in which the hobbyist may receive a financial benefit in addition to the benefit conferred by the hobby itself. Of all the hobbies, only the collectables offer their pursuers psychological satisfaction as well as pecuniary gain; and of the collectables, none offers more of both than stamps.

INVESTMENT ADVISERS

As stamps become a viable investment, it is natural that a variety of specialized investment advisers have grown up. If you subscribe to some of the stamp newspapers and magazines listed in the bibliography, you will see the advertisements for these; other investment advisers are beginning to solicit clients on the business pages of local newspapers and in the financial press. It is very difficult to ascertain the expertise of any of these advisers. Like economists, these people must make predictions based on inadequate knowledge about the future. And further, even an excellent record of predictions in the past is no guarantee of success for the future. Generally, philatelists who have done the best in stamps have done so because they themselves have acquired a good measure of philatelic knowledge. Some choose to use the investment advisers as well, but prudence would seem to dictate giving no one carte blanche with your money.

Philatelic Organizations

~~~~~~

It is hard to imagine a more organized group of people than stamp collectors. There are tens of thousands of local philatelic clubs, and probably over a thousand large-scale organizations worldwide. Some of the large ones are listed below. All clubs welcome new members in the spirit of international friendship and cooperation. After all, that's what stamp collecting is all about. By writing to any of the following organizations, a collector can find out what the membership procedure is.

American Philatelic Society, Box 800, State College, PA 16801. The largest collectors' society in the United States, with over 50,000 members. A host of services are available for a modest membership fee. A free brochure is sent on request. Every collector should belong—their monthly magazine, *The American Philatelist,* is excellent.

Society of Philatelic Americans, Box 904, Wilmington, DE 19809. Originally developed in the 1890s as a southern alternative to the American Philatelic Society, the SPA used to stand for Southern Philatelic Society. The name was changed in 1922, and today the SPA is a national society. Smaller than the APS, but offering much the same services.

American Topical Association, 3306 N. 50th Street, Milwaukee, WI 53216. A large organization, devoted to the promotion of topical or thematic philately, it is made up of people who simply collect, say, cats on stamps, or complicated aero-philately, or arctic exploratory themes. Offers much the same services as the above two national societies, but with a topical twist.

The Collectors Club. This is a small society, based in New York, made up of America's most serious collectors. Their magazine, *The Collectors Club Philatelist,* is a technical journal. There are two meetings a month, and nonresidents are encouraged to join, if only to get the magazine. Information is available from the Collectors Club, 22 E. 35th Street, New York, NY 10016.

American Stamp Dealers Association. ASDA membership is limited to stamp dealers who pledge to a strict code of ethics. Dealing with the ASDA members is a collector's surest guarantee of fair play. Information on members is available from ASDA, 840 Willis Avenue, Albertson, NY 11507.

Annotated Bibliography

~~~~~~

This book has only touched on numerous aspects of postal history and philately. Some other books and periodicals well worth consulting are listed below.

UNITED STATES

Antrim, E. *Civil War Prisons and Their Covers* (New York: Collectors Club, 1961). A historically oriented study of Civil War prisoners of war.

Armstrong, Martin A. *The Washington Family Heads of 1908–1921* (Trenton, N.J.: Trenton Publishing Company, 1977). These stamps are presently very popular, and this is a capable book about a complex issue.

Ashbrook, Stanley B. *The U.S. One Cent Stamp of 1851–57* (New York: H. L. Lindquist, 1938). Published in two volumes, this is the finest philatelic work in English. It is the study of only one stamp, but through it Ashbrook explains American postal emissions and history during its most formative years. Before the middle of this century, there was never the high degree of philatelic specialization that is so prevalent today. Ashbrook's book marks the turning point of this specialization, which was brought about by price inflation in philately. The book is a work of genius.

Blake, Maurice, and Davis, Wilbur. *Postal Markings of Boston, Massachusetts to 1890* (Lawrence, Mass.: Quarterman Publications, reprinted 1973). A 360-page book on the postal history and markings of one town. Probably too awesome for a wide audience, but it shows how expansive a seemingly small philatelic subspecialty can be.

Blazer, Clarence. *Essays for U.S. Adhesive Postage Stamps* (Lawrence, Mass.: Quarterman Publications, reprinted 1977). "Essays" are produced designs that are never issued. This catalogue lists most of the American ones, though it gives no prices.

Brookman, Lester. *The U.S. Postage Stamps of the Nineteenth Century* (New York: H. L. Lindquist, 1967). A three-volume tour de force, this is the bible of classic U.S. philately. Out of print a decade now and due for a reprint, the book is so useful that collectors gladly fork out $200 or more when one comes on the market.

Chase, Carroll. *The Three Cent Stamp of the United States, 1851–57 Issue* (Lawrence, Mass.: Quarterman Publications, reprinted 1976). Long a classic, this book has fortunately been reprinted. Dr. Chase was one of the greatest students of American stamps, but his writing tends to be a little frigid. For specialists only.

Dietz, A. *The Postal Service of the Confederate States of America 1928* and *Confederate States Catalog and Handbook 1959* (Richmond, Va.: Dietz Publishing Co., 1959). The major works on Confederate philately. The issues of the Confederate States of America were not touched on in this book because of space limitations. They are, however, fascinating stamps that are avidly collected by many Americans.

Gobie, Henry M. *The Speedy: A History of U.S. Special Delivery* (Miami, Fla.: Wilhelmina M. Gobie, 1976). An excellent work on United States Special Delivery Stamps (the E #s).

———. *U.S. Parcel Post—a Postal History* (Miami, Fla.: Wilhelmina M. Gobie, 1979). Another excellent work by Gobie. And both books are still in print!

Hargest, George E. *History of Letter Post Communication Between the United States and Europe 1845–1875* (Lawrence, Mass.: Quarterman Publications, reprinted 1971). This book details the postal arrangements on transatlantic mails during the mid-nineteenth century. Since its publication some fifteen years ago, it has spurred tremendous collector interest in postage rates and routings of letters.

Johl, Max. *U.S. Stamps of the Twentieth Century* (Lawrence, Mass.: Quarterman Publications, reprinted in one volume 1976). Originally published in four volumes, to 1935 when the series stopped. This is a highly detailed, invaluable study by a great scholar. Most researchers still turn to Johl, though the work is sometimes too detailed even for many specialists.

Lidman, David. *The Treasury of Stamps* (New York: Harry N. Abrams, 1976). A beautifully photographed, lovingly written book on postage stamps—but of course we are prejudiced in favor of the author.

Luff, J. N. *Postage Stamps of the U.S.* (New York: Scott Stamp and Coin Company, 1902). This work, published by the aging Luff in 1902, represents the facts as collected by one of America's greatest philatelists, who had the good fortune to live most of his life during the period in which the greatest philatelic history was being made. The book is long out of print and hard to find, but a philatelist should at least glance at it, as it is the foundation on which much modern knowledge about U.S. stamps rests.

Neinken, M. *The U.S. One Cent Stamp 1851–61* (Canton, Ohio: U.S. Philatelic Classics Society, Inc., 1972). An update of Ashbrook, with important new plating information.

———. *The United States Ten Cent Stamps of 1855–59* (New York: Collectors Club, 1960). Another important specialized contribution by one of America's most skilled modern philatelic students.

Planty, Earl. *U.S. First Day Cover Catalog of Classic Cachets, 1923–1933* (Coral Springs, Fla.: Earl Planty, 1974). In the early days of first-day cover collecting, there was great competition between the different cachet makers and a host of beautiful colorful cachets resulted, most of which are avidly collected to this day. This catalogue lists and explains them. Planty was one of the pioneers in this branch of collecting.

Remerle, C. W. *U.S. Railroad Postmarks 1837–1861* (State College, Pa.: The American Philatelic Society, Inc., 1958). For years during the nineteenth century, railroad stations maintained post offices and applied their own distinctive cancellations, usually using the station name and the initials "R.P.O." for Railroad Post Office. This book lists the different cancellations for the period. Some are very common; others are unique. Collecting R.P.O. cancellations (nearly always done on cover) was much more popular twenty years ago, when the railroads were a more important influence on American life than they are today. *See also* Towle and Meyer.

Sloane, G. B. *Sloane's Columns* (West Somerville, Mass.: Bureau Issues Association, 1961). George Sloane wrote a column in *Stamps Magazine* for about thirty years. This is a compilation of his pieces, arranged by topic (though unfortunately not indexed). Sloane was a brilliant, kindly man, who knew his field (U.S. philately) intimately. He is said to have written the best column on his deathbed; to his credit, it is just as pointed as his first.

Thorpe-Bartels. *U.S. Stamped Envelopes* (Netcong, N.J.: Prescott Holden Thorp, 1968). A two-volume catalogue of United States Postal Stationery stamped envelopes, listing them not only by die type (as the Scott catalogue does—see p. 57) but also by knife (cut of the envelope) and watermark of the paper. The result is that Thorpe-Bartels gets thousands of varieties where Scott gets only hundreds. This specialty requires patience, good eyes, and more than an average amount of concentration, but its rewards are an occasional rarity hauled out of a philatelic dustbin.

Toppan, Deats, and Holland. *Historical Reference List of Revenue Stamps of the United States* (Lawrence, Mass.: Quarterman Publications, reprinted 1980). Nobody liked this title, so they call it the *Boston Revenue Book*. First published in 1899, it was long out of print and sold for hundreds of dollars. Recently, it was republished at an exceedingly modest price, considering that this has a wealth of information on early U.S. revenue issues.

Towle and Meyer. *Railroad Postmarks of the United States* (Canton, Ohio: U.S. Philatelic Classics Society, Inc., 1968). The companion volume to Remerle, discussed above.

United Postal Stationery Society. *Catalog of Postal Stationery of U.S. Possessions* (Albany, Ore.: Van Dahl Publications, 1971). A valuable resource for stationery collectors.

———. *U.S. Postcard Catalog* (Bloomington, Ill.: United Postal Stationery Society, 1975). A large and detailed catalogue of U.S. postal cards.

Walcott, G. *Civil War Patriotic Covers* (New York: Robert Lawrence, 1934). This is actually an auction catalogue, albeit a large one, from the 1930s. Walcott's collection was such a comprehensive one that it is hard to find a legitimately used design that is not in his catalogue.

CANADA

Boggs, W. S. *Postage Stamps and Postal History of Canada* (Lawrence, Mass.: Quarterman Publications, reprinted 1975). The definitive study of Canadian stamps, by a great scholar. Over 600 pages long, recently reprinted, it gives all of the historical background of Canada's postal affairs, along with a detailed discussion of the stamps, listing all of the major varieties.

Holmes, L. S. *Specialized Philatelic Catalogue of Canada and British North America.* This work is a little out of date (especially the pricing), but it prices items that are listed nowhere else. And you can use a form of extrapolation to update the prices.

Lyman's Standard Catalogue of Canada and British North America Postage Stamps. This is a little pocketbook listing all the Canadian issues of general interest (Canada and Great Britain are listed in Vol. I of the Scott catalogue with the rest of the British Commonwealth).

BRITISH COMMONWEALTH

Stanley Gibbons British Commonwealth Catalogue. The British equivalent to the Scott catalogue. And like Scott, Gibbons is strongest in its home country.

Lowe, Robson. *The Encyclopedia of the British Empire.* Available from H. J. M. R. Co., Box 6638, Hollywood, Florida 33021. A five-volume work, first appearing in 1948 and still being issued. It has a profound postal history slant. This is a fantastic book—the British Commonwealth collecting area is fortunate to have Lowe.

———. *The British Postage Stamps of the Nineteenth Century.* A fine overview of the period leading up to the issuance of postage stamps.

WORKS OF MAJOR IMPORTANCE ON FOREIGN STAMPS

Virtually every specialized area of philately, be it China or Chile, has its own works and catalogues. In this section, we have listed works that because of the quality of philatelic scholarship do more than simply illuminate their subject. They are also a beacon showing philatelists exactly how fine research should be done. Note that philatelic French or German is very like philatelic English. Once you master fifty basic nouns and verbs, plus fifty technical philatelic terms (which you wouldn't have learned in high-school language class anyway), following any foreign specialized catalogue is not too difficult. There are thousands of philatelic books on thousands of subjects. Readers interested in establishing a philatelic library should contact H. J. M. R. Co., Box 6638, Hollywood, Fla. 33021.

Austria

Mueller, Edwin. *Postmarks on Definitive Issues of the Austro-Hungarian Empire* (in German). Literally thousands of postmarks are listed and priced. The first issue of Austria is very common—probably the most readily available imperforates in the world. And the wealth of cancellations makes this a marvelous collecting field. A comprehensive book, worthy of adulation.

Ferchenbauer—Austria Catalogue. A highly specialized catalogue of the stamps of Austria, and Bosnia and Herzegovina.

Tschilingarian and Stephen. *The Austrian Post Offices Abroad.* The Austrians had post offices abroad, much like the Americans, English, and French. This is a six-volume comprehensive catalogue.

Curaçao

Julsen, Frank W., and Benders, A. M. *The Postal History of Curaçao.* A 600-page postal history of a tiny island, this book has been two decades in the making. It exhaustively researches all the stamps and even the postmarks (helped by the fact that the Dutch kept postal records for Curaçao that are the envy of postal historians all over the world).

France

Yvert & Tellier. *Catalogue of the Stamps of France* (in French). Yvert & Tellier is to France what Scott is to the United States, the general catalogue producers. In 1975 they issued a large, hardbacked specialized study and catalogue of the nineteenth-century stamps of France. This volume had been promised for years. And they advised that Volume II, covering the twentieth century, would be out shortly—we are still waiting. When it comes out, if you have the vaguest interest in French philately, buy it. Volume I, like most good philatelic books, was issued in a very limited quantity, sold out quickly, and now commands a substantial premium. The book is in French, but is so replete with pictures that anyone can follow it.

Germany

Michel—The Specialized Catalogue of Germany (in German). The Germans have applied their usual thoroughness to philately. German stamps have been studied backwards and forwards; not only do the Germans collect many stamps, depending on where the watermark falls on them, they also, on the Colonial issues, count the perforations on the stamps to spot rarities too minute to show up on a perforation gauge. The catalogue is well laid out—a wondrous amount of information is crammed into about 360 pages.

Grobe, H. *Catalogue of German States* (in German). Before 1870 and the beginning of the consolidation of the German Empire, what we now call Germany was actually a number of different countries, united by a common language and mutual enemies. Baden, Bavaria, Hamburg, Prussia, Saxony, and various other areas issued their own postage stamps. Grobe is a specialized catalogue of these stamps. The Scott catalogue gives a good overview but does not mention that because these stamps were completely demonitized in the 1870s no effort was made to enforce anticounterfeiting laws against people who made copies of them. Forgeries are common, though less so now than fifty years ago. Most German forgeries, especially the ones sold between 1880 and 1920, went as such to people who could not afford the originals and simply wanted to fill the spaces. The owner knew he had forgeries, but that information is long forgotten when the collection is found in some attic by relatives who now imagine themselves to be fabulously wealthy. "Don't worry about these stamps," we hear from the finders. "This collection is ninety years old." That's just when we do worry! Buy German States stamps only from knowledgeable experts.

Guatemala

Goodman, R. A. *The Postal History and Philately of Guatemala* (2 volumes). A thorough work, assembling virtually all the important philatelic knowledge of Guatemala. These two volumes have made Guatemalan philately the most popular Central American philately. Too often, most of the knowledge in a country is published here and there in magazine articles, then lasts only as long as the best recall of one of its readers. The Guatemala work assembled this information and put it all in one accessible place.

Israel

Bale. *Catalogue of Palestine and Israel.* A 240-page specialized catalogue of Israeli stamps, in English.

Italy

Sassone. *Italy Specialized Catalogue.* A large, specialized catalogue. Like Germany, Italy until the late nineteenth century was an amalgamation of states, all of which issued their own stamps.

Japan

Woodward, T. *Postage Stamps of Japan and Dependencies.* A 726-page reprint of one of the great philatelic classics. Detailed and worth having. More specialized, but an achievement of no less magnitude is Dr. Ichida's *The Dragon Issue* (first issue) and *The Cherry Blossom Issue.* Forgeries of these early stamps are common, made just a few years after the real stamps for stamp collectors. Dr. Ichida's contribution enables us quickly to separate the wheat from the chaff.

Scandinavia

Facit. *The Scandinavian Specialized Catalogue.* The specialized catalogue for Denmark, the Faroe Islands, Greenland, Danish West Indies (with the American Virgin Islands), Finland, Iceland, Norway, and Sweden.

Switzerland

The Zumstein Catalogue. An annual specialized catalogue listing covers, multiples, perforations, and specialty material that Scott does not give.

In a general vein, L. N. and M. Williams's *Fundamentals of Philately* (State College, Pa.: The American Philatelic Society, Inc., 1971) is an extremely comprehensive study of printing, gumming, and papermaking. This book is highly thought of by many philatelists.

STAMP PERIODICALS

In addition to the magazines published by the major philatelic organizations (see p. 227), the following weekly publications are useful:

Linn's Stamp News, P.O. Box 29, Sidney, Ohio 45367.

Stamp Collector, P.O. Box 10, Albany, Ore. 97321.

Index

Illustrations are *italicized*.

address codes, 15
airmail issues (U.S.), *61,* 154–58, *157, 159, 160, 209*
  inverted, 155, 191–96, *192–93,* 197, 202
Alice in Wonderland stamp case, *54*
Amelia Earhart stamp (Mexican), *217*
American Bank Note Company, 121, 182, 183–84
American Philatelic Expertization Service (APES), 72
American Philatelic Society (APS), 72, 227
American Stamp Dealers Association (ASDA), 71–72, 228

American stamps. *See* United States stamps
American Topical Association, 228
approval sales, 59
Archer, Henry, 162–63, 164
Ashbrook, Stanley, 28
Atherton Shift, 101–2
August issues, 1861 (U.S), 100–101

bank notes, *78*
  collection of, 45, 125
  sets of, 120–23, *122, 124, 126*
beaver, on three penny (Canadian), *175,* 177, *178*
Blackjack. *See* two cent, 1861 (U.S.)
Blue Nose, 1929 (Canadian), *211*

British Guiana, One Cent Magenta
of, 197–200, *198,* 217
British postal history
fraud in, 14–16
rates in, 13–14
reform in, 16–18
stamp invention and, 18–21
British Postal Reform Act (1839),
19
British Post Offices Abroad, 169–
70
British stamps
cancellations on, 162, *169*
colors of, 161–62
design duration of, 164–65
with double thread line, 164
1883 issue of, *171*
1887–92 issue of, *172*
embossed issues of, 164, *165*
with four check letters, 166–68
of high values, *169,* 170
Edwards, *173*
initial designs for, 19–21, *20*
introduction of, 18–19, 161
1913–19 issue, *174*
reuse prevention for, 110
separation of, 162–63
in early perforated issues, 163,
164, *165*–66
surface-printed, 168–69
unseparated, 33–34
Used Abroads, 169–70
watermarks on, 31, *32*
Brookman, Lester, 115
Bureau of Engraving and Printing
(BEP), stamps of, 141–44,
145
Burrus, Maurice, 200

cachet, defined, 46
calendar collection, 92
Canadian stamps, 31, 32
Blue Nose (1929), *211*
collectors and collecting of, 186–
87
in decimal currency issue (1854),
178–79

Dominion issues of (1868–70),
180–81, *182*
early issues of, 175–78
Edward VII issue (1903) of,
185, *187*
George V (1912), *190*
Imperial Penny Postage issue
(1898) of, 184–85, *185, 186*
Jubilee issue (1897) of, 182, *183*
on laid and wove paper, 176–77
Maple Leaf issue (1897) of,
183–84, *184*
perforations on, 177–78
Quebec Tercentenary issue
(1908) of, 186, *188, 189*
cancellations
with circle date stamp (CDS),
91–92, 103
cleaning of, 80–81, 110
collection of, 91–92, 103, *104,
105*
handstamped, *12*
Hiogo, 108
target, 177, *181*
Cape of Good Hope triangulars,
23, *25,* 42
Carroll, Lewis, postage-stamp case
design of, *54*
Centennial Exposition (1875),
reissues and special printings
at, 127, 129–32, *129, 130,
131, 132, 133*
centering, 35, 116
certification process, 72–73
chalky paper, 110
Chase, Carroll, 28
China
postal history in, 8
U.S. postal agency in, *130*
Christmas, 1898 (Canadian), 185,
186
Church, medieval postal service of,
2–3
circle date stamp (CDS)
cancellation, 91–92, 103
Civil War
postal history in, 99–100, 106

stamp issues of, 100–109
Collectors Club, The, 228
color shift, 196
Columbian Exposition issues
    (1893), 43–44, *136–37*
    on first-day covers, 138–39
    post office profiteering and, 136–
        37
    prices of, 138, 139
commemorative stamps, 45, *48*, 138
    *See also specific stamps and
        issues*
communications
    ancient, 1–2
    future of, 11–12
    postal system development in, 2–
        10
Continental Bank Note Company,
    121, 125
corner cards, 33
cover, defined, 45–46
creases, 62–63
    repair of, 65
Cross grade stamp, 61–62

Danish stamps, 36
dealers
    complaints against, 71–72, 73
    price lists of, 58, 156
    selection of, 70–71
    stamp buying through, 60
Declaration of Independence
    (Trumbull), on twenty-four
        cent (1869), 117–18
Demmy, Roger, 217–19
Depression of 1929–39, stamp
    prices in, 213
die proofs
    large, *25*
    progressive, *26*
double paper, 110
double transfers, *29*, 89, 101–2,
    181
dry stamps, 4, *5, 6, 7*
Dutch Indies stamps, fugitive inks
    on, 110–11

Edward VII (King of England)
    on British issues, *173*
    on Canadian issues, 185, *187,
        188*
eight cent, 1901 (U.S., Pan
    American), 147
Elizabeth II (Queen of England),
    183
engraving methods, 24, 27
envelopes
    advertising on, *83*
    commemorative, *17*
    first-day covers, 138–39, 224
    Mulready, 18, 33, *34, 39*
    patriotic, 106
    See also cancellations; letters,
        early
Extremely Fine grade stamp, 61

face scrapes, 62
Fair grade stamp, 60–61
faults
    detection of, 63–64
    repair of, 64–65
    types of, 62–63
Ferrary, Philipp La Renotiere von,
    43, 199
fifteen cent
    1861 (U.S.), 113
    1869 (U.S.), 115–17
Fine grade stamp, 61
first-day covers, 45–46, 138–39,
    224
five cent
    1847 (U.S.), 76–78, *79*, 128
        reproduction of for Centennial
            Exposition (1875), 127, *129*
    1851 (U.S.), 84–85
    1857 (U.S.), 94–95, *131*
    1859 (Canadian), *178*
    1861 (U.S.), 107
        grill types of, 112, 113
    1901 (U.S., Pan American), 147
    1902 (U.S.), *150, 152*
five dollar
    1893 (U.S., Columbus), 98–99

1894–95 (U.S., Bureau issues),
    141–42, 143
1902 (U.S.), *150,* 152
flat press, 69
four cent
    1898 (U.S., Transmississippi),
        144, *145*
    1901 (U.S., Pan American), 147,
        149
    1902 (U.S.), *150,* 152
franking privilege, *16*
    abolition of, 17
    postal fraud and, 15–16
Franklin, Benjamin
    autograph of, *76*
    on U.S. issues, *77, 115,* 154
Free Frank, *16,* 17
    fraud in, 15–16
French stamps, collectors and
    collecting of, 38
fugitive ink, 110–11

George V (King of England)
    on British issues, *174*
    on Canadian issues, *188, 190*
German stamps, *210*
Gibbons, Edward Stanley, 40, 42,
    57
Giroux, Hector, 205
gold, investment in, 208, 210
Good grade stamps, 60–61
Great Britain. *See* British postal
    history; British stamps
Green, Ned, 195
grill types
    on bank notes, 121
    forgeries of, 114–15
    identification of, 111–15
gum
    application of, 35–36, 65
    originality of, 66–68
    removal of, 36
gummed tabs, 55

Hawaiian Missionaries, 203–5
Herpin, George, 38
Hill, Rowland, *17,* 19, 33

on perforated stamps, 34, 162
postal reform and, 16–18
Hind, Arthur, 200
hinges, peelable, 56
Hiogo cancellations, 108

imperforate stamps, 152
Imperial Penny Postage
    (Canadian), 184–85, *185*
    Christmas (1898), 185, *186*
Imperial Postal Conference of
    1898, 184
Inca postal system, 8
inverted stamps, *116,* 117, 118,
    119, 147, *148*
    airmail, 1918 (U.S.), 155, 191–
        96, *192–93,* 197, 202
investment
    in gold, 208, 210
    in nineteenth century, 207–8
    in stock market, 208
    See also stamp investment
Ishakawa, Royohei, 205
Italian states, postal service
    development in, 3–5

Jackson, Andrew, on two cent
    (1861), 101
Japanese stamps
    early, *27*
    investment in, 218
Jamestown issue, 1907 (U.S.),
    153–54
Jubilee issue, 1897 (Canadian),
    182, *183*

Klein, Eugene, 194–95

laid paper, 28, 31, 176–77
Large Queen issue, 1868
    (Canadian), 180
Leroux, Gaston, 204
letters, early
    cancellation on, *12*
    with dry stamp, *5, 6, 7*
    nineteenth century, *14*
    free franked, *16*

by ship post, *11*

Lindbergh airmail, 156, *158*

line engraving, in stamp printing, 24, 116

Linn's World Stamp Almanac, 228

Louisiana Purchase issue, 1904 (U.S.), 152–53, *153*

Luff, John, 43

McKinnon, N. R., 199

Maltese Cross cancellation, 162

Maple Leaf issue, 1897 (Canadian), 183–84, *184*

Mauritius
    one- and two-penny stamps of, *23,* 201
    Post Office issue of, 201–2

Mexican stamps, Amelia Earhart in, *217*

mint stamps, collecting of, 40, 66, 139, 186

Moens, Jean-Baptiste, 40, 66, 202

mounting, 68
    with gummed tabs, 55
    with peelable hinge, 56
    with plastic mounts, 56–57

Mulready envelope, 18, 19, 33, *34, 39*

mutual fund, stamp investment by, 214

National Bank Note Company, 121, 125, *126*
    1861 essays of, 100–101

never hinged (NH) stamps, 67

nibbed perforations, 68–69

Nicaragua, stamps of, 44

nine pence, 1862 (British), 168

ninety cent
    bank note (U.S.), *123, 124, 126*
    1857 (U.S.), 96–99, *97, 98*
    1861 (U.S.), 109, 113–14
    1869 (U.S.), 118, *120*

Nyassa Company stamp, *50*

one cent
    British Guiana Magenta, 197–200, *198,* 217

1851 (U.S.), 28, 82–84, *90–91*

1857 (U.S.), 89–90
    reissue of, 127, *131*

1859 (Canadian), *178*

1861 (U.S.), 101

1868 (Canadian), 180

1869 (U.S.), 115

1901 (U.S., Pan American), 147, *148*

1902 (U.S.), *150, 152*

one dollar, 1898 (U.S., Transmississippi), 144

one-half penny, 1855 (Canadian), 177

One Penny (British), 166
    1841, *162, 163,* 164–65
    1864, 164–65, 166–68, *167*
    See also Penny Black; Penny Red

OSTROPA, 1936 (Germany), 36

Pan American Exposition issue, 1901 (U.S.), *63,* 146–49, *146, 148,* 152
    first-day cover of, 138–39

paper
    chalky, 110
    double, 110
    flaws in, 62–65
    pelure, 204
    wove and laid, 28, 31, 176–77

papermaker watermarks, 32–33

patent cancels, 110

Patriotic envelopes, 106

pelure paper, 204

Penny Black, 21, 161
    design of, *21,* 22
    printing of, 24, 27

Penny Red, 161–62

perforating machine, 35, 163, 164, 177–78

perforations
    defined, 34
    errors in, 196
    first issues with, 35, 164, 165–66
        Canadian, 178
        U.S., 88–99
    gauge of, 68

stamp quality and, 68–69
  with straight edges, 69–70
Perkins, Bacon & Petch, 166, 168
Perot stamp, *29*
Philatelic Foundation (PFC), 72,
  73
philately
  derivation of, 38
  See also stamp collectors and
    collecting
plastic stamp mount, 56–57
plating work, 28
Pony Express, 93
Poor grade stamps, 60–61
postage stamps. *See* stamp(s)
postal history
  church messengers in, 2–3
  fraud in, 14–16
  of Italian states, 3–5
  pre-Renaissance, 1–2, 8–9
  University of Paris Post in, 2
  See also British postal history;
    United States postal history
Postal History Division of History
  and Technology Museum,
  Smithsonian, 135
postal stationery, 164
Post Office Fresh, 67
*Post Office Reform, Its Importance
  and Practibility* (Hill), 16

Quebec Tercentenary issue, 1908
  (Canadian), 186, *188, 189*

railway post office cancellations, 92
rare stamps, *23, 39, 94, 96*
  through design error, 197
  double transfer as, *29*
    Atherton Shift, 101–2
  Hawaiian Missionaries, 203–5
  inverts, *116,* 117, 118, 147, *148*
    airmail, 1918 (U.S.), 155,
      191–96, *192–93,* 197, 202
  as investment, 214–15, 219
  One Cent Magenta (British
    Guiana), 197–200, *198,* 217
  through perforation error, 196
  price of, 202

quantity issued and, 150–51
Rawdon, Wright, Hatch & Edson,
  76, 175, 178
Reagan, John, 99–100
reentries, 181
Regular issues, 1861 (U.S.), 100
Renaissance, postal history of, 3–5
Ridpath, Thomas, 199
Robey, William, 191, 194, 195
Roman post roads, 8
rotary printing, 69
rouletting, 34–35, 163
Rumanian stamps, *24*

Salvador, stamps of, 44
Scott, J. Walter, 40–41
Scott catalogue, 57, *58*
  numbering system of, 75–76
*Scott Standard Postage Stamp
  Album,* 40
Sea Horses, *174*
secco marks, 4, *5, 6, 7*
Seebeck, Nicholas F., 44
se-tenant, *31*
Sforza, Francesco (Duke of Milan),
  3
Sierra Leone, stamps of, *25*
six cent
  1869 (U.S.), 115
  1918 (U.S., airmail), 154
six penny, 1851 (Canadian), 175
sixteen cent, 1918 (U.S., airmail),
  154–55
Small, Frederick, 200, 216–17, *218*
Small Queen issue, 1870
  (Canadian), 180–81, *182*
Society of Philatelic Americans
  (SPA), 72, 228
Society for the Suppression of
  Spurious Stamps (SSSS), 136
stamp(s)
  albums for, 49–50, *50–51, 52*
  catalogs of, *41,* 57–58
  auction, 59–60
  certification of, 72–73
  design of, 22–23
  die proofs of, *25, 26*
  dry, 4, *5, 6, 7*

errors on. *See* rare stamps
faults in, 62–64
forgeries of, 42, 164
grades of, 60–62, 71
  centering in, 35
gum on, 35–36
  originality of, 66–68
hand, *24*
handling of, 212
identifier for, 53, *55*
invention of, 18–19
mint, 40, 66
paper for. *See* paper
pictorial, 115
plating of, 27–28
printing methods for, 23–24, 27,
    66–67, 69
  in two colors, 116
repair of, 64–65
reuse of, 110–11
separation methods for, 34–35,
    162–63
  See also perforations
straight edge, 69
tax, *19*
toned, 154
tongs for, 53, 55
watermarks on, 31–33
*See also specific countries and
    types*
stamp collectors and collecting
  in approval sales, 59
  at auctions, 59–60
  basic supplies for, 49–55
  of bank notes, 125
  of Canadian stamps, 186–87
  of cancellations, 91–92, 103,
    104, 105
  characterized, 49, 115, 216–19,
    225
  through dealers. *See* dealers
  development of, 40, 42
  of first-day covers, 138–39, 224
  future of, 225–26
  in Great Britain, 170–71
  of high-value stamps, 143
  of hinged and never hinged
    stamps, 67

  for investment, 219–20, 221
  of mint stamps, 40, 66, 81, 139
  motivation for, 47, 48–49
  mounting methods in, 55–57, 68
  national issues for, 44
  for novice collection, 51–52
  numbers of, 47–48
  organizations for, 227–28
  origins of, 37–38
  of perforated and nonperforated
    stamps, 68–70
  of post-1890 period, 134
  specialization in, 45
  thematic, 46
stamp investment, 52–53
  advisers for, 226
  first-day covers and, 224
  through mutual funds, 214
  new issues and, 223–24
  personal styles of, 216–19
  price shopping and, 215–16
  pros and cons of, 212–15
  recommended countries for, 224–
    25
  returns on, 221–23
  strategies for, 219–21
stamp prices, 45
  in catalogues, 57–58
  dealers' price lists on, 58
  in Depression, 213
  increase rate for, 210–11, 222
  of mint *vs* used stamps, 139, 186
  of no gum *vs* original gum
    stamps, 67–68
  for rarities, 202
    airmail invert, 197, 202
    Mauritius Post Office issue,
      202
    One Cent Magenta, 199–200,
      217
Steele, Charles, 111
stitch watermarks, 32
stock market investment, 208
Superb grade stamp, 61
supplementary mail, cancellation
    of, *92*
surface-printed stamps, 168–69

Tapling, T. K., 43
Tappan, Carpenter & Company,
   88, 89
target cancel, 177, *181*
Taxis postal system. *See* Thurn
   and Taxis postal system
tax stamp, *19*
tears, 63
   repair of, 65
ten cent
   1847 (U.S.), 76–77, 78, *80, 81,
      128*
      reproduction of for Centennial
         Exposition (1875), 127, *130*
   1851 (U.S.), 86–87
   1854 (Canadian), 179
   1857 (U.S.), 95
   1859 (Canadian), *179*
   1861 (U.S.), 107, 113
      Japanese cancellation on, 108
   1869 (U.S.), 115
   1898 (U.S., Transmississippi),
      144, 145
   1901 (U.S., Pan American), 147
   1904 (U.S., Louisiana
      Purchase), 152–53
ten pence
   1855 (Canadian), 177, *179*
   1867 (British), 169
thins, 62
   filling of, 64–65
thirteen cent, 1902 (U.S.), 150–51
thirty cent
   bank note, *132*
   1857 (U.S.), 96, *97*
   1861 (U.S.), 109
      grill types of, 112, 113
   1869 (U.S.), *115*, 118, *119*
three cent
   bank note, *122*, 125
   1851 (U.S.), 84
   1857 (U.S.), 90–92
   1861 (U.S.), 102–3, 106
      cancellations on, 103, *104, 105*
      grill types of, 112, 113, 114
   1868 (Canadian), 180
   1869 (U.S.), 115

1904 (U.S., Louisiana
   Purchase), 152–53
three penny, beaver (Canadian),
   175, 177, *178*
Thurn and Taxis postal system, 5,
   9–10
   rates of, *10*
   routes of, *9*
Thurn and Taxis stamps (1852),
   30
Tiffany, John, 43
Timbremania, 38
tongs, use of, 53, 55
topical collections, 46
Transmississippi issue, *68*, 144,
   144–45
triangular stamps, 23, *25*
twelve cent
   1851 (U.S.), 87, *88*
   1857 (U.S.), 95, *96, 131*
   1861 (U.S.), 108, *109*, 113, 114
   1869 (U.S.), 115
twelve ½ cent (Canadian), *179*
twelve penny, 1851 (Canadian),
   175, 176
twenty-four cent
   bank note, *123*, 125
   1857 (U.S.), 96, *97, 131*
   1861 (U.S.), 109, 113
   1869 (U.S.), *115*, 117–18
   1918 (U.S., airmail), 155
two cent
   Hawaiian Missionary, *203*,
      204–5
   1861 (U.S.), 101
      double transfer on, 101–2
      grill type of, *113*, 114
   1868 (Canadian), 31, 180
   1869 (U.S.), 115
   1901 (U.S., Pan American),
      138–39, 147, *148*
two dollar, 1902 (U.S.), *150*, 151–
   52
Two Penny (British)
   Blue, *161*, 162
   1841, 162, *163*

United States postal history, 75
  in Civil War, 99–100, 106
  fraud in, 15
  Pony Express in, 93
  western expansion and, 92–93
United States stamps
  airmail issues of, 61, 154–58,
      157, 159, 160, 209
    inverted, 155, 191–96, *192–
      93,* 197, 202
  in bank notes, 45–46, 120–25,
      122, 124, 126
  in Bureau issues, 141–44, *145*
  Columbian Exposition issues of,
      43–44, 136–40, *136–37*
  1851 issues of, 81–87
  1857 issues of, 88–99, 127, 129–
      30, *131*
  1861 issues of, 100–109, 130,
      132
  1869 issues of, 115–20, 132
  1890 issues of, *134,* 135
  first issues of, 75–81, *79*
    cleaned cancellations on, 80–
      81
    posted from Canada, 78
  grill types of, 111–15
  imperforate, 152
  Jamestown issue of, 153–54
  living persons on, 156–57
  Louisiana Purchase issue of,
      152–53, *153*
  1902 issue of, 149–52, *150*
  Pan American Exposition issue
      of, 146–49, *146, 148,* 152

  perforated, 88
  printing methods for, 69, 116
  reissues of, 126, 129–32
  reuse prevention for, 110–11
  special printings of, 132, *133*
  of twentieth century, 146, 154
  watermarks on, 31–32, 141–42
  See also rare stamps; *specific
      names and types*
University of Paris, early postal
    system of, 2

Very Good grade stamp, 61
Victoria (Queen of England), 183
  on British issues, *21, 22,* 38,
      161–63, 165, 167–69, 171–72
  on Canadian issues, 180–82,
      183, 184, 185

Washington, George, on U.S.
    issues, 86–87, *88,* 154
watermarks
  on Bureau issues, 141–42, 143
  determination of, 64
  types of, 31–33
watermark tray, 64
  use of, 65
women
  as collectors, 37–38
  on U.S. issues, 153
wove paper, 28, 31, 177
Wyon, William, 21
Wyon City Medal (1837), *21*

zeppelin stamp, 158, *159, 160, 209*